Center Pieces

A Cookbook from the | Cultural Arts League
Gadsden, Alabama

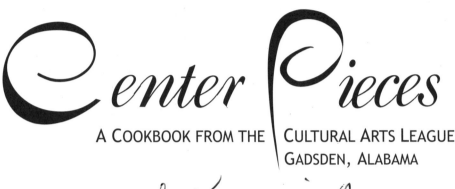

To: Cathy
Happy Entertaining
Best Wishes
Benny Campbell

Merry Christmas
2000!
Debbie

Mission Statement

The Cultural Arts League supports the Center for Cultural Arts in Gadsden, Alabama by serving as official hostesses, providing cultural enrichment, encouraging others to become members and supporting fundraisers on behalf of the Center.

Dedication

Center Pieces is dedicated to those individuals who have given untiringly to improve the quality of life in Northeast Alabama by their continued support of the Center for Cultural Arts.

On The Cover: The Basil Gilchrist Memorial Fountain located in the Center for Cultural Arts Courtyard. As the dedication plaque reads, "This fountain salutes the life and memorializes Basil Gilchrist, truly a man for all seasons. His contributions to the civic and cultural life of our city and state are legion."

Published by The Cultural Arts League,
Center for Cultural Arts,
P.O. Box 1507, Gadsden, AL 35902

© 2000 by the Cultural Arts League

ISBN: 0-9702062-0-8

This cookbook is a collection of favorite recipes, which are not necessarily original recipes. Liberties have been taken to ensure consistency of form.

The proceeds realized from the sale of *Center Pieces* will be used exclusively to benefit the Center for Cultural Arts.

Printed in the USA by

WIMMER
The Wimmer Companies
Memphis
1-800-548-2537

The Gadsden Times *is a*

proud supporter of community

events, charities and activities.

We are proud to have had a

role in helping the Cultural

Arts League support area

cultural activities by assisting

with the design of Center Pieces.

Special thanks go to newsroom graphic artist Laura Bentley.

The Gadsden Times

Attalla
Florist

Special Thanks to
Benny Campbell of Attalla Florist
for creating the floral arrangements
found throughout Center Pieces.

Cookbook Committee

Chairman
Phyllis Young Cordell

Recipe & Editorial Chairmen
Suzy Haller
Susan Harwood
Marcy Puckett
Heather Rickles
Julie Waldrup

Committee
Deirdre Coakley
Charlotte Cohn
Miki Cook
Jeanne Dozier
Carolyn Hawkins
Pudden McArthur
Sheila McCorkle
Mariella McNair
Tracy Miller
Rebecca Noojin
Maxine Rosser
Janet Russo
Joanie Sledge
Thea Woodliff

Gadsden Cultural Arts Foundation Board Liaison
Marsue Lancaster

Contributors

A special thanks to the members of the Cultural Arts League, their families and friends who provided cherished recipes for *Center Pieces*. We regret that we were unable to include all recipes submitted due to similarity or availability of space. Publication of this book would not have been possible without the dedication and support of all those who submitted recipes, cooked, hosted testings, evaluated dishes, proofed recipes, loaned props and photographed the centerpieces.

A (*) denotes members of the Cultural Arts League 1996 to 2000.

Joyce Allen *	Liz Dailey	Jo Ellen Hardy
Mack Allen *	Florence Daugette	Mandy Hartzog
Rita Allen *	Sara Dickson	Susan Harwood *
Judy Atkins	Loucille Dolberry	Beppy Hassey
Karen Baltz *	Jeanne Dozier *	Carolyn Hawkins *
Laura Bentley	Gann Duke	Chad Hawkins
Sandra Berman *	Terry Duke	Fran Hawkins *
Wendy Brasher *	Betty Echols	Suzanne Habyan
Jackie Brechin	Katie Eiland *	Carrie Heath
Jacqueline Brehm *	Rebecca Follo	Prudence Hilburn
Diane Brown	Brenda Ford	Connie Hill
Grace Brown	Gadsden Service Guild	Lisa Hogan
Louise Brown	Mike Gagliardo	Heidi Holt
Shirleen Brown	Kay Gibbs	Ira Holt
Donna Burgraf *	Kim Gibson *	Iris Isbell
Helen Burke	Kathy Graf *	Ben Johnson *
Katherine Burke *	Sara Graf	Corella Johnson
Celeste Cedarholm	Marcy Gregerson	Roscoe Johnson
Nancy Chazen	Katie Grimes	Becky Kampakis
Sallie Christopher	Kathy Gross	Heidi Karod *
Charlotte Cohn *	Clarice Haller	Paula Keck
Mary Faye Cohn *	Helene Haller	Joan Kerr *
Miki Cook *	Suzy Haller *	Faye Kilpatrick
Phyllis Cordell *	Barbara Hagedorn *	Marsue Lancaster *
Robert Crabtree	Betty Hammond	Jane Lane
Joanna Culp *	Elisabeth Hardin *	Debbie Leach * ⚔
Ann Cummans *	Montine Hardin	Joan Leach *

Katherine Pike Lee

Susan Little

Judi Loveman

Burt Lowe

Mary Malone

Clara Martin

Pudden McArthur *

Molly McCartney

Sheila McCorkle *

Pat McDaniel

Kathy McFarland *

Susan McGuire

Charlotte McKenzie *

Don McNair

Mariella McNair *

Mayor Steve Means

Gayden Metcalfe

Tracy Miller *

Vickie Mitchell

Tee Morgan

Ellen Morris *

Gayla Murdock

Jane Newman *

Bernadette Nickson

Julie Nolen

Rebecca Noojin *

Carolyn Norman

Shirley Northcutt *

Helen O'Loughlin *

Karen Owen

Wayne Owen

isha Pace *

Rick Paler

Donna Patterson

Jane Patton *

Harriet Phillips

Mae Phillips

Bille Faye Picht *

Vicky Porter

Jennifer Powers *

Karen Puckett

Marcy Puckett *

Joanne Ray *

Anne Renfrow *

Clare Renfrow

Ray Renfrow

Marie Rice

Kay Richardson

Heather Rickles *

Jessica Robertson

Diane Rogerson

Maxine Rosser *

Katherine Rowe *

Janet Russo

Serendipity Dance Club

Sylvia Saltz *

Camelle Sasser *

Suzann Scharfenberg *

Miriam Shannon

Pat Sherman

Melissa Shields

Reynolds Shook

Cynthia Sirna

Joanie Sledge *

Nancy Smith *

Nan Spivak *

Donna Stassinis *

Sylvia Stewart *

Vicki Street

Jan Sutton

Mia Taylor *

Evelyn Terrell

George Terrell

Eloise Turk *

Julie Tysver

Jeanne Vance

Karen Vanore *

Melissa Waldron *

Cathy Waldrup

Julie Waldrup *

Kathy Warren

Herstyne Watson

Bobby Welch

Pat Welch

Nancy Wells

Peggy Wetzel *

Bill Willard

Joy Williams *

Mary Jo Williams

Valerie Williams-
Pennington

Thea Woodliff *

Hazel Worden

Mary Young *

Ruth Young

Special thanks to Roger Hawkins, Ron Reaves, Laura Bentley and others from The Gadsden Times *for their invaluable assistance in making* Center Pieces *a reality.*

ecial thanks also to Deirdre Coakley and Sheila McCorkle for their proofreading assistance.

The Center for Cultural Arts

A Short History

During the 1980s, negative media attention thrust the city of Gadsden, located in Northeast Alabama, into the national spotlight. A Rand McNally report ranked Gadsden as one of the nation's ten worst U.S. places to live. When city officials inquired how a town located along a scenic riverway, surrounded by mountains and rich in traditions could garner such a negative recognition, they learned that one of the reasons was a zero in the arts and culture category.

The arts were not completely missing from Gadsden. There were active theatre companies, music organizations and other arts-related groups, but city leaders knew the community needed an arts "center" - a place where the arts would be visible, accessible to citizens and of interest to visitors. It was to be located in the deteriorating downtown and also serve as a spur to revive the historic district.

The Gadsden Cultural Arts Foundation, became the engine of arts development.

Preston Phillips, A.I.A., a Gadsden native who had become a prominent architect based in New York, agreed to design his hometown's new art center. He transformed a former department store building to include three exhibition halls, art studios, meeting rooms, offices, restaurant facilities and a breath-taking atrium over the original escalators. Using stark black and white with a gold shingled cylinder overlooking Broad Street, the building itself became a piece of art.

In January 1990, an elaborate gala marked the opening of the Center for Cultural Arts and the beginning of a new era. The 44,000 square-foot facility, along with the river and mountains, had become a permanent part of the Gadsden landscape.

By 1999, the Foundation's original vision of exhibition halls and some meeting rooms grew to include a cityscape of 1940's Gadsden with a 72-foot model train installation, a children's museum, the Etowah Youth Orchestras, musical and theatrical productions, and the Gadsden Community School for the Arts.

Gadsden has now been recognized both as one of "America's most livable cities" by the National League of Cities and as an "All-American City" by the National Civic League.

The Cultural Arts League

Supporting the Arts

When the Center opened, it quickly became the heart of the community. Volunteers were needed to help the small staff expand services, so in 1996, the Cultural Arts League was formed. It is comprised of community-minded people of all ages who share a common interest in the arts and the well-being of the Center. League members support the Center by holding a highly anticipated annual auction. Proceeds from the auction have been used to pay for renovations to the adjacent Kyle Building, home of Imagination Place Children's Museum. The League helps organize the Center's docent program, decorates the Center for the holidays, sponsors a chair in the Etowah Youth Orchestra and hosts the elegant receptions held at the opening of new exhibitions.

The Cookbook Project

Soon after the League began hosting artists' receptions, members began receiving compliments on the welcoming atmosphere and the delicious, beautifully presented food. A cookbook presented an opportunity to raise funds for Center projects.

League members and other volunteers spent hours preparing, testing and sharing recipes. Every week for months, a cookbook committee member hosted a dinner or lunch at her home. Other League members attended, each preparing a dish from the hundreds of recipes that were submitted. Husbands, Foundation board members, friends and neighbors were all called on to try recipes as deadlines approached.

Center Pieces tells the story of the Center for Cultural Arts by using each chapter to describe a "Piece" of the whole. The title also lends itself to exploring the art of entertaining by presenting unique floral arrangements. For this the League turned to Attalla Florist owner, Benny Campbell, who is nationally recognized for the artistic expression found in his arrangements. He was as enthusiastic about the the project as the League.

It didn't take long to decide to use artist to transform photographs of Campbell's work into paintings. For the cover, Nikki Hogan, an up-and-coming local artist, captured the details of the beautiful Basil Gilchrist Memorial Fountain located in the Center courtyard.

Jay Tysver, who was introduced to the League through *The Gadsden Times*, a New York Times Company newspaper, brought life and color to the inside of the book with his interpretations of the arrangements. *The Gadsden Times* staff also created the page design and were instrumental in seeing the project come to fruition.

For everyone on the committee, publishing this book has truly been a labor of love. We are proud of the result, and hope that you not only enjoy preparing and serving the recipes that follow, but also learn more about the Center for

Cultural Arts. We invite you to visit the Center soon and take advantage of its many programs.

✴ Benny Campbell

Floral designer Benny Campbell is well-known for his work at weddings and other gala events across the South. Campbell is owner of Attalla Florist and Design, located in Gadsden's sister city, Attalla, Alabama.

His masterpieces have been recognized by national publications and pictured in *Southern Accents, Southern Bride, People* magazine and several issues of *I Do . . . for Brides*. He has also been a featured designer for the annual "Art in Bloom" exhibit at the Birmingham Museum of Art and for numerous decorator showhouses.

Campbell graduated from Auburn University with a degree in landscape design and ornamental horticulture, with a concentration in floral culture. Campbell travels the country lecturing, conducting workshops and leading class tours to flower markets in destinations like New York and London.

Nikki Hogan

A Steele, Alabama native, Nikki Hogan took private lessons from Gadsden artist Elaine Campbell for three years before pursuing a career in painting and drawing at Gadsden State Community College. Ms. Hogan's mentor, GSCC professor of art, Dennis Sears, introduced her to the Cultural Arts League just months before she began the final stage of work on her bachelor's degree in fine art at Montevallo University in Montevallo, Alabama.

Already recognized for her realistic paintings and figurative drawings, Ms. Hogan has accepted many commissions including her favorite to date - the Basil Gilchrist Memorial Fountain that appears on the cover of *Center Pieces*.

Jay Tysver

After receiving a bachelor's degree in graphic arts from Florida State University, Jay Tysver began his career as a spec artist with the New York Times Company and then continued to improve his illustration skills by working as a news artist. Since 1994, Mr. Tysver has worked for the New York Times Company as a pre-press manager with *The Gadsden* (Ala.) *Times* and the (Florence, Ala.) *Times Daily*.

The paintings Mr. Tysver created for *Center Pieces* challenged his skills as an artist. Known for his sports portraitures, the *Center Pieces* project was an opportunity to work with subject matter like stems and petals of flowers and the surfaces of a variety of foods. Along with his work for the New York Times Company, Mr. Tysver frequently takes commissioned work and is always painting for his own enjoyment.

Table of Contents

Shrimp and Grits

Southerners in the Low-Country of Georgia and South Carolina grow up eating this classic for breakfast.

1 tablespoon olive oil
½ pound smoked sausage, cut in half lengthwise and sliced into ½-inch pieces
2 teaspoons chopped garlic
2 pounds medium shrimp, peeled and deveined
Salt and freshly ground pepper to taste
¼ cup dry sherry
2 cups shrimp stock or clam juice
4 tablespoons cold butter
2 teaspoons chopped fresh parsley
Creamy Stone Ground Grits (see page 20)
Garnish: parsley

▸ Heat olive oil in large skillet at medium temperature.
▸ Add sausage and cook 2 minutes. Add chopped garlic, cook 30 seconds.
▸ Season shrimp with salt and pepper to taste. Add shrimp to skillet. Cook 4 minutes, or until shrimp turn pink.
▸ Remove skillet from the heat, add sherry. Return to the stove and flame the sherry, shaking skillet gently until the sherry flames out.
▸ Remove the shrimp and sausage from the skillet with a slotted spoon. Set aside.
▸ Add the stock to the skillet and bring to a boil, cook until sauce is reduced to about 1 cup. Lower the heat to medium low and add 4 tablespoons cold butter, one tablespoon at a time, whisking constantly. Return the shrimp and sausage to the skillet. Simmer just until hot. Remove from heat and stir in 2 teaspoons chopped parsley.
▸ Divide grits into 8 bowls. Spoon shrimp mixture over grits.
▸ Garnish with parsley.
Yield: 8 servings

Grillades and Grits

This New Orleans version of steak, served over grits and smothered in rich gravy, makes an inexpensive supper or a grand, old-fashioned breakfast.

1½ pounds round or veal steak cut ½-inch thick
½ teaspoon salt
¼ teaspoon pepper
2 tablespoons all-purpose flour
2 to 3 tablespoons vegetable oil, divided
½ cup minced onion
½ cup chopped green onions
1 garlic clove, minced
3 tablespoons chopped fresh parsley
1 tablespoon chopped green bell pepper
1 cup canned diced tomatoes, undrained
1 to 1½ cups beef broth
Grits Timbales or Grits Timbales Variation (see page 21)

▸ Trim steak and season with salt and pepper; dust both sides with flour and pound with a meat mallet. Cut into bite-size pieces.
▸ Cook steak in 2 tablespoons hot oil in a Dutch oven over medium heat until browned on all sides. Remove from Dutch oven and set aside.
▸ Add more oil to Dutch oven, if necessary, and sauté minced onion, green onions, and garlic in hot oil, stirring occasionally, until onion is translucent and lightly browned.
▸ Return steak to Dutch oven and add parsley, bell pepper, and tomatoes. Add enough broth to cover.
▸ Bake covered at 325° for 1 hour and 30 minutes to 2 hours or until meat is tender, stirring occasionally and adding broth as needed for desired consistency.
▸ Remove from oven and skim off fat. Serve over hot cooked grits.
Yield: 4 to 6 servings

Chicken Strata Soufflé

This works equally well for dinner.

3 tablespoons butter or margarine
½ cup chopped onion
½ cup chopped celery
3 cups diced cooked chicken
½ cup mayonnaise
Salt and pepper to taste

1 (4-ounce) jar diced pimiento, drained
6 white bread slices, cubed
4 large eggs, lightly beaten
2 cups milk
1 (10¾-ounce) can condensed cream of mushroom soup, undiluted
1½ cups (6 ounces) shredded cheddar cheese

▸ Melt butter in a medium skillet over medium heat; add onion and celery. Sauté until onion is translucent. Remove from heat and add chicken, mayonnaise, salt and pepper to taste, and pimiento, stirring well.
▸ Place half of bread cubes in the bottom of a greased 13 x 9 x 2-inch baking dish; spoon half of chicken mixture over bread. Repeat layers.
▸ Combine eggs and milk, stirring well; pour over chicken mixture. Spread mushroom soup over top of casserole.
▸ Bake at 350° for 1 hour, or until set in the middle.
▸ Remove from oven and sprinkle with cheese. Bake 10 more minutes or until cheese is melted.

Yield: 6 to 8 servings
NOTE: If desired, cover and chill 8 hours or overnight. Remove from refrigerator and let stand, covered, at room temperature for 1 hour before baking.

Sausage and Egg Casserole

"A favorite of my children and their friends. It was always requested for after-dance breakfasts."

6 white bread slices, torn into bite-size pieces
1 (8-ounce) package Old English cheese slices, torn into bite-size pieces
¾ pound ground pork sausage, cooked and drained
¼ cup butter or margarine, melted
4 large eggs, lightly beaten
2 cups milk
½ teaspoon salt
½ teaspoon dry mustard

▸ Arrange bread and cheese in alternate layers in a greased 13 x 9 x 2-inch baking dish; pour butter over top. Sprinkle evenly with sausage.
▸ Combine eggs, milk, salt, and mustard in a bowl, stirring well; pour over layers in baking dish. Cover and chill 8 hours or overnight.
▸ Remove from refrigerator and let stand, covered, at room temperature 1 hour before baking.
▸ Bake at 350° for 1 hour or until set in the middle.

Yield: 8 servings

Cheese Puff

Rich, creamy, and easy to prepare with refrigerated crescent rolls.

2 (8-count) packages refrigerated crescent rolls
2 (8-ounce) packages cream cheese, softened
¾ cup sugar
1 teaspoon vanilla extract
1 tablespoon fresh lemon juice
1 large egg, separated
1 cup seedless preserves, heated (optional)
1 tablespoon water

▸ Unroll dough and press 1 package into the bottom of a 13 x 9 x 2-inch baking dish, pressing seams to seal.
▸ Beat cream cheese, sugar, vanilla, lemon juice, and egg yolk at medium speed with an electric mixer until creamy; pour over dough in baking dish.
▸ Spread preserves over cream cheese mixture, if desired. Top with remaining package of roll dough, gently pressing seams to seal.
▸ Combine egg white and 1 tablespoon water, stirring well; brush over dough.
▸ Bake at 350° for 25 minutes or until lightly browned.
Yield: 12 servings

Baked French Toast

Great for Christmas morning or when you have houseguests.

1 (12-ounce) French bread loaf, cut into ½-inch slices
½ cup butter or margarine, melted
1 cup firmly packed brown sugar
1 teaspoon ground cinnamon
6 large eggs
2 cups milk
Maple syrup

▸ Place 1 layer of bread slices as close as possible in a greased 13 x 9 2-inch baking dish.
▸ Combine butter, brown sugar, and cinnamon; spread sugar mixture over bread slices. Cover with remaining bread slices.
▸ Combine eggs and milk in a bowl, stirring well; pour over bread. Cover and chill overnight.
▸ Remove from refrigerator and let stand at room temperature 30 minutes.
▸ Bake, covered, at 350° for 20 to 25 minutes; uncover and bake 10 to 15 more minutes. Remove from oven and drizzle syrup over top; broil until brown and bubbly.
Yield: 6 to 8 servings

Artichoke and Mushroom Strata

Vegetarian breakfast casserole

1 tablespoon butter
1 cup fresh mushrooms, sliced
½ cup thinly sliced green onions
2 cups Italian or French bread cubes
¾ cup (3 ounces) shredded Swiss cheese
1 (14-ounce) can artichoke hearts, drained and quartered
1 (4-ounce) jar diced pimiento, drained
4 large eggs
1½ cups milk
½ teaspoon dry mustard
½ teaspoon salt
½ teaspoon pepper
½ teaspoon dried Italian seasoning (optional)

▸ Melt butter in a large skillet over medium-high heat; add mushrooms and green onions and sauté 4 to 5 minutes or until tender.
▸ Place half of bread cubes in the bottom of a greased 10-inch deep-dish pie plate or 2-quart baking dish. Layer half each of mushroom mixture, cheese, artichoke hearts, and pimiento. Repeat layers.
▸ Whisk eggs until light and fluffy; add milk and remaining ingredients, mixing well. Slowly pour egg mixture over vegetable layers. Cover and chill 8 hours or overnight.
▸ Remove from refrigerator and let stand, covered, at room temperature 1 hour before baking.
▸ Bake, uncovered, at 350° for 45 to 60 minutes or until set and lightly browned.
▸ Let stand at room temperature 10 minutes before serving.

Yield: 6 servings

NOTE: This recipe can be doubled to serve 12. Cook in a 13 x 9 x 2-inch baking dish.

Spinach and Pistachio Quiche

A delectable treat for your favorite guests

1 unbaked 10-inch pastry shell
3 large eggs, lightly beaten
1 cup whipping cream
½ cup ricotta cheese
1 teaspoon salt
¾ teaspoon chopped fresh dill or ½ teaspoon dried dill weed
¼ teaspoon ground white pepper
¼ teaspoon sugar
½ cup (2 ounces) shredded Swiss cheese
1 tablespoon grated fresh Parmesan cheese
¾ cup chopped spinach, cooked and drained
¼ cup pistachios, shelled and finely chopped
1 cup (4 ounces) shredded provolone or Swiss cheese
Paprika to taste

▸ Line pastry shell with aluminum foil and fill with rice, dried beans, or pie weights.
▸ Bake at 400° for 7 minutes. Remove from oven and remove weights and foil. Let cool on a wire rack.
▸ Combine eggs, whipping cream, ricotta, salt, dill, pepper, and sugar in a bowl, stirring well. Stir in Swiss and Parmesan cheeses, spinach, and nuts. Pour into prepared pastry shell.
▸ Bake at 350° for 40 to 45 minutes or until firm. Remove from oven and sprinkle with provolone or Swiss cheese and paprika. Bake 4 to 8 more minutes or until cheese is melted.

Yield: 6 servings

Eggs in Ramekins with Creamed Chicken

Luxurious taste and texture

4 tablespoons butter, divided
2 tablespoons all-purpose flour
1 cup chicken broth
Ground red pepper to taste
2 cups cubed cooked chicken breast (½-inch cubes)
Salt and pepper to taste
¾ cup whipping cream, divided
⅛ teaspoon freshly ground nutmeg
12 large eggs

- Melt 2 tablespoons butter in a heavy saucepan over medium heat; whisk in flour. Cook, whisking constantly, 1 minute.
- Add broth and cook, whisking constantly, until thickened and smooth. Season with red pepper to taste. Add chicken, salt and pepper to taste and cook, stirring gently, 1 minute. Stir in ¼ cup whipping cream and nutmeg and cook until thoroughly heated.
- Lightly grease 12 (4-ounce) ramekins or custard cups with remaining 2 tablespoons butter.
- Spoon 2 tablespoons creamed chicken in each ramekin; break an egg over each and top each with 2 teaspoons whipping cream. Sprinkle with salt and pepper to taste.
- Arrange ramekins in a large pan; fill pan with boiling water halfway up ramekins.
- Bake at 400° for 10 to 12 minutes or until egg whites are firm and yolks are soft.
- Do not overcook. Serve in ramekins.

Yield: 12 servings

Toasted Egg Cups

Let your children help you make these.

6 white bread slices (very fresh)
2 tablespoons butter, melted
6 large eggs, lightly beaten
¼ cup milk
1 teaspoon salt
¼ cup (1 ounce) shredded sharp cheddar cheese

▸ Cut crusts from bread and discard. Brush both sides of bread with melted butter. Gently press bread slices into 6 large custard cups.
▸ Combine eggs, milk, salt, and cheese in a bowl, stirring well with a fork. Pour ⅓ cup egg mixture into each bread cup.
▸ Place custard cups in a shallow pan.
▸ Bake at 350° for 30 minutes.
Yield: 6 servings

Creamy Stone Ground Grits

Stone ground whole grain grits are available at most health food stores.

2 cups stone ground whole grain grits
2 cups milk
2 cups water
1 teaspoon salt
Freshly ground black pepper to taste
½ cup butter
½ cup (2 ounces) grated white cheddar cheese

▸ Soak and drain grits according to package directions.
▸ Combine milk, water, salt, pepper and ½ cup butter in saucepan over medium heat.
▸ Bring to a boil and gradually stir in grits. Reduce heat to medium low and cook 1 hour until grits are tender and creamy, stirring every 10 minutes to prevent sticking. Add additional water during cooking process to keep creamy.
▸ Remove from heat, stir in cheese. Season with additional salt and pepper if .needed. Keep warm.

Grits Timbales

Today grits are flavored with herbs and cheese, baked in custard cups, and inverted on a "pool" of savory sauce for an impressive dinner presentation.

6 cups water
1½ cups uncooked grits
2 teaspoons salt
2 garlic cloves, minced
1½ cups (6 ounces) shredded sharp cheddar cheese
4 tablespoons grated Parmesan cheese, divided
½ teaspoon salt
½ teaspoon freshly ground pepper
3 egg yolks, lightly beaten
½ cup whipping cream

‣ Bring 6 cups water to a boil in a Dutch oven; add grits and salt and cook according to package directions. Remove from heat and stir in garlic, cheddar cheese, 2 tablespoons Parmesan cheese, salt, and pepper.
‣ Combine egg yolks and whipping cream, stirring well; stir into grits.
‣ Spoon grits into 12 (4-ounce) buttered ramekins. Place ramekins in a large pan and pour hot water to a depth of 1 inch in pan. Cover with aluminum foil.
‣ Bake at 350° for 30 minutes. Remove from oven and let cool.
‣ Remove timbales from ramekins; place upside down on a greased baking sheet. Sprinkle with remaining 2 tablespoons Parmesan cheese.
‣ Broil 5 inches from heat 3 minutes or until browned.
Yield: 12 servings
VARIATION: For casserole, spoon grits mixture into a greased 13 x 9 x 2-inch baking dish. Bake at 350° for 45 minutes or until set. Remove from oven and sprinkle with Parmesan cheese; bake 4 to 8 more minutes or until lightly browned.

Blintz Cheese Torte

Lightly sweetened cheese torte - perfect for a brunch

Crust
1 (6-ounce) package zwieback
½ cup sugar
1 teaspoon ground cinnamon
½ cup butter or margarine, melted

▸ Process zwieback in a food processor until finely ground. Add sugar, cinnamon, and butter, processing until blended. Reserve ¾ cup mixture and press remaining mixture in the bottom and up the sides of greased springform pan.

Filling
1½ pounds cottage cheese
4 large eggs
1 cup sugar
⅛ teaspoon salt
Grated rind and juice of 1 lemon
1 teaspoon vanilla extract (optional)
1 cup cream
¾ cup all-purpose flour
½ cup almonds or pistachios, finely chopped

▸ Process cottage cheese in a food processor until smooth. Pour through cheesecloth to strain, discarding liquid.
▸ Beat eggs at medium speed with an electric mixer until lemon colored; add salt, lemon rind, lemon juice, and, if desired, vanilla, beating well.
▸ Add cream, cottage cheese, and flour, beating well.
▸ Pour Filling into crust.
▸ Combine reserved ¾ cup crumb mixture and almonds or pistachios; sprinkle over Filling.
▸ Bake at 325° for 1 hour.
▸ Turn off oven and let cool in oven at least 1 hour. Open oven door and let cool 30 more minutes.
▸ Remove from oven and let cool completely on a wire rack. Chill.
▸ Remove sides of springform pan to serve.
Yield: 1 (9-inch) torte

Hot Fruit Compote

A versatile recipe - as good for brunch as it is for supper

1 (29-ounce) can sliced peaches in light syrup
1 (20-ounce) can pineapple chunks in juice
2 (15-ounce) cans applesauce, divided
3 teaspoons ground cinnamon, divided
1 (15¼-ounce) can apricot halves
1 (16½-ounce) can seeded purple plums
1 (15-ounce) can pineapple slices in juice
1 (16½-ounce) can Bing cherries
1 (8-ounce) can green grapes

▸ Drain all fruits well.
▸ Layer peach slices, pineapple chunks, and 1 can applesauce in a
  13 x 9 x 2-inch baking dish; sprinkle with 1 teaspoon cinnamon.
▸ Slice apricot halves and plums and arrange over applesauce; top with
  remaining can of applesauce. Sprinkle with 1 teaspoon cinnamon.
▸ Arrange pineapple slices, cherries, and grapes over applesauce; sprinkle
  with remaining 1 teaspoon cinnamon.
▸ Bake at 350° for 1 hour to 1 hour and 30 minutes or until bubbly.
  Spoon off any juices that come to the top.
Yield: 10 to 12 servings

Carrot Cake Muffins

Great with luncheon salads

1 cup all-purpose flour
1 tablespoon baking powder
¼ teaspoon salt
1 teaspoon ground cinnamon
2 cups wheat bran cereal
1 cup skim milk
1½ cups shredded carrot
⅓ cup firmly packed brown sugar
1 large egg, lightly beaten
2 tablespoons vegetable oil
⅓ cup raisins

▸ Coat muffin pan with vegetable cooking spray.
▸ Combine first 4 ingredients in a large bowl.
▸ Combine cereal and milk in a separate bowl; let stand 3 minutes. Add carrot, brown sugar, egg, and oil to cereal mixture, stirring well.
▸ Add cereal mixture to flour mixture, stirring just until dry ingredients are moistened (batter will be lumpy). Stir in raisins.
▸ Spoon batter into greased muffin pan cups, filling each cup two-thirds full.
▸ Bake at 400° for 25 minutes or until a wooden pick inserted in center comes out clean. Serve warm.
Yield: 1 dozen

Currant Scones

Enjoy the rich, buttery flavor of this Scottish treat.

3 cups all-purpose flour
2½ teaspoons baking powder
½ teaspoon baking soda
¾ teaspoon salt
⅓ cup sugar
¾ cup butter, cut into pieces
1 cup buttermilk
¾ cup currants
1 teaspoon grated orange rind
1 tablespoon whipping cream
¼ teaspoon ground cinnamon
2 tablespoons sugar

- Combine first 5 ingredients in a bowl; cut in butter with a fork or pastry blender until mixture is crumbly.
- Add buttermilk, currants, and orange rind, stirring just until dry ingredients are moistened. Form dough into a ball, pressing so it holds together.
- Turn dough out on a lightly floured surface and knead 12 times; divide into 2 portions and pat each portion into a ½ to ¾-inch thick circle.
- Cut each circle into 8 pie-shaped wedges and place slightly apart on an ungreased baking sheet.
- Combine heavy cream, cinnamon, and 2 tablespoons sugar in a small bowl, stirring well. Brush dough with glaze.
- Bake at 400° for 12 to 15 minutes or until tops are browned. Serve hot.

Yield: 16 scones

Orange Muffins

These yummy glazed muffins are great for a tea party.

2 cups all-purpose flour
1 teaspoon baking soda
½ teaspoon salt
1 cup raisins
½ cup pecans, chopped
1⅓ cups sugar, divided
Grated rind and juice of 1 orange
2 large eggs, lightly beaten
1 cup buttermilk
½ cup butter, melted

- Grease muffin pan.
- Combine first 5 ingredients, 1 cup sugar, and orange rind in a large bowl, stirring well. Make a well in the center of the mixture.
- Combine eggs, buttermilk, and butter in a small bowl, stirring well; pour into well and stir just until dry ingredients are moistened.
- Spoon batter into greased muffin pan, filling each cup two-thirds full.
- Bake at 350° for 25 to 30 minutes or until a wooden pick inserted in center comes out clean. Remove muffins from pan and let cool on a wire rack.
- Bring orange juice to a boil in a small saucepan over medium heat; add remaining ⅓ cup sugar and cook, stirring often, until sugar is dissolved. Brush or spoon glaze over warm muffins.

Yield: 1 dozen

Mocha-Chocolate Chip Muffins

A great surprise for overnight guests

1 teaspoon boiling water
4 teaspoons instant coffee granules
2 cups self-rising flour
½ cup granulated sugar
1 teaspoon ground cinnamon
2 large eggs
½ cup milk
¼ cup vegetable oil
¼ cup firmly packed brown sugar
¾ cup semi-sweet chocolate morsels
Streusel Topping

- Coat muffin pans with vegetable cooking spray.
- Combine 1 teaspoon boiling water and coffee granules, stirring until dissolved. Set aside and let cool.
- Combine flour, granulated sugar, and cinnamon in a medium bowl, stirring until blended.
- Combine coffee mixture, eggs, milk, oil, and brown sugar in a small bowl, whisking until blended. Add to flour mixture, stirring just until dry ingredients are moistened (batter will be lumpy; do not over mix). Fold in chocolate morsels.
- Spoon batter into greased muffin pans, filling each cup two-thirds full. Sprinkle each with 1 tablespoon Streusel Topping, pressing lightly into batter.
- Bake at 375° for 8 to 12 minutes or until a wooden pick inserted in center comes out clean.
- Remove from oven and let cool on wire racks 5 minutes. Remove from pans and let cool completely on wire racks.

Yield: 1½ dozen

Streusel Topping
3 tablespoons butter, softened
¼ cup firmly packed brown sugar
1 teaspoon ground cinnamon
½ cup chopped almonds
¼ cup self-rising flour

- Combine first 3 ingredients in a small bowl, stirring until smooth.
- Add nuts and flour, stirring until mixture is crumbly.
- Sprinkle on Danish, coffee cakes, muffins, or cinnamon rolls before baking.

Yield: about 1 cup

Date Cake Muffins

"My mother's muffins are as good for a dessert buffet as they are for breakfast."

1 cup chopped dates
1 cup boiling water
1 tablespoon margarine
1 teaspoon baking soda
1 cup granulated sugar
1 large egg, lightly beaten
1½ cups all-purpose flour
¼ teaspoon salt
1 teaspoon vanilla extract
1 cup chopped nuts
Powdered sugar
Cream cheese (optional)

▸ Grease miniature muffin pans.
▸ Combine dates and 1 cup boiling water in a large bowl; stir in margarine and baking soda. Let cool 10 minutes.
▸ Add granulated sugar, egg, flour, salt, and vanilla to date mixture, beating well with a wooden spoon. Stir in nuts.
▸ Spoon batter into greased miniature muffin pans, filling each cup two-thirds full.
▸ Bake at 375° for 15 minutes or until a wooden pick inserted in center comes out clean. Remove muffins from pan and let cool completely on wire racks.
▸ Sprinkle muffins with powdered sugar and serve with cream cheese, if desired.

Yield: 4 dozen

Cranberry-Nut Bread

Superb! A good bazaar bread

1 cup fresh or frozen cranberries, coarsely chopped
½ cup chopped nuts
1 tablespoon grated orange rind
2 cups all-purpose flour
1½ teaspoons baking powder
½ teaspoon baking soda
1 teaspoon salt
1 cup sugar
2 tablespoons shortening
¾ cup fresh orange juice
1 large egg, lightly beaten

▸ Lightly grease 9 x 5 x 3-inch loaf pan.
▸ Combine first 3 ingredients in a small bowl, stirring well.
▸ Combine flour, baking powder, baking soda, salt, and sugar in a large bowl; cut in shortening with a fork or pastry blender.
▸ Combine orange juice and egg; add to flour mixture, stirring just until dry ingredients are moistened. Fold in cranberry mixture.
▸ Pour batter into greased loaf pan.
▸ Bake at 350° for 1 hour or until a wooden pick inserted in center comes out clean. Remove from oven and let cool on a wire rack 15 minutes. Remove from pan and let cool completely on wire rack.

Yield: 1 loaf

Banana Bread

Moister than your average banana bread

3 cups self-rising flour
1½ teaspoons baking powder
1½ teaspoons baking soda
2 cups sugar
¾ cup vegetable oil
2 large eggs
1⅛ cups buttermilk
½ teaspoon vanilla extract
1½ cups mashed banana
1 cup chopped pecans or walnuts

- Grease 7 (3½ x 6¼-inch) loaf pans.
- Combine flour, baking powder, and baking soda in a bowl.
- Beat sugar and oil at medium speed with an electric mixer until creamy; add eggs, beating well.
- Add flour mixture to creamed mixture alternately with buttermilk, beginning and ending with flour mixture and beating after each addition. Add vanilla, banana, and nuts, beating just until blended.
- Pour batter into greased loaf pans - no more than ⅔ full.
- Bake at 350° for 30 minutes or until a wooden pick inserted in center comes out clean. Remove to a wire rack and let cool 10 minutes. Remove from pans and let cool completely on wire rack.

Yield: 7 small loaves

Light Banana-Nut Bread

"It's as good as the high-fat version." For rich flavor and tender texture, use very soft bananas with brown spotted peels.

1 cup mashed very ripe banana (about 3 small)
½ cup sugar
½ cup plain nonfat yogurt
¼ cup margarine, melted
1 teaspoon vanilla extract
1 large egg
1 egg white
2 cups all-purpose flour
1 teaspoon baking powder
½ teaspoon baking soda
¼ teaspoon salt
¼ cup chopped pecans, toasted

- Coat an 9 x 5 x 3-inch loaf pan with vegetable cooking spray.
- Beat first 7 ingredients at medium speed with an electric mixer until well blended.
- Combine flour, baking powder, baking soda, and salt; stir in pecans. Add to banana mixture, stirring just until dry ingredients are moistened.
- Spoon batter into greased loaf pan.
- Bake at 350° for 1 hour and 5 minutes or until a wooden pick inserted in center comes out clean. Remove from oven and let cool 10 minutes on a wire rack; remove loaf from pan and let cool completely on wire rack.

Yield: 1 loaf

Apricot Bread

A tasty tea bread to take to a friend

1 cup dried apricots, finely chopped (6 ounces)
½ cup pecans, chopped
2 cups all-purpose flour, divided
2 tablespoons butter or margarine, softened
1 cup sugar
1 large egg
2 teaspoons baking powder
¼ teaspoon baking soda
1 teaspoon salt
½ cup orange juice
¼ cup water

▸ Grease the bottom of 2 (3½ x 6¼-inch) loaf pans or 1 (9 x 5 x 3-inch) loaf pan. Line the bottom with wax paper. Grease the paper and set aside.
▸ Soak the chopped apricots in hot water for 20 minutes. Drain and set aside.
▸ In a large bowl combine the melted margarine and sugar. Cream well and add egg, thoroughly blend. Stir in water and orange juice.
▸ Combine flour, baking powder, baking soda and salt in a small bowl. Add to egg mixture. Beat until blended. Add apricots and nuts; blend well. Pour batter into pan(s). Let stand for 20 minutes.
▸ Bake at 350° (for small pans, bake for 55 to 60 minutes; for large pan, bake 1 hour or until a wooden pick inserted in center comes out clean).
▸ Cool in pan on wire rack 5 minutes; remove from pan and immediately remove waxed paper. Cool.

Yield: 2 loaves

Sticky Buns

"So easy, children can do this with a little help from Mom."

½ cup chopped walnuts or pecans
2 tablespoons raisins (optional)
1 (25-ounce) package frozen homestyle roll dough, not thawed
1 (3.5-ounce) package butterscotch pudding mix (not instant)
6 tablespoons butter or margarine, melted
½ cup firmly packed brown sugar
1 teaspoon ground cinnamon

▸ Grease a 10 x 3½-inch Bundt pan.
▸ Sprinkle nuts and, if desired, raisins in bottom of pan.
▸ Arrange frozen roll dough evenly over nut mixture; sprinkle with pudding.
▸ Combine butter, brown sugar, and cinnamon; pour over dough.
▸ Cover and let rise in a warm place (85°), free from drafts, 8 hours, overnight or until dough rises to the top of the pan.
▸ Bake at 350° for 30 minutes or until lightly browned, covering with aluminum foil after 15 to 20 minutes if necessary to prevent overbrowning.
▸ Remove from oven and let cool on a wire rack 5 to 10 minutes. Turn out onto a serving plate with a rimmed edge and serve.

Yield: 12 servings

Mexican Coffee Cake

You can do the first step the night before and finish it up in the morning.

2½ cups all-purpose flour
½ teaspoon salt
1 cup firmly packed brown sugar
¾ cup sugar
¾ cup vegetable oil
2 tablespoons ground cinnamon
½ cup chopped pecans
1 teaspoon baking soda
1 teaspoon baking powder
1 large egg, lightly beaten
1 cup buttermilk
½ cup butter, melted (optional)

▸ Combine first 6 ingredients in a large bowl. Remove ¾ cup mixture and add pecans, stirring well. Set aside.
▸ Grease a 13 x 9 x 2-inch pan.
▸ Add baking soda, baking powder, egg, and buttermilk to remaining batter, stirring well (batter will have small lumps).
▸ Pour batter into greased pan and sprinkle nut mixture over top.
▸ Bake at 350° for 20 minutes. Remove from oven. If desired, drizzle melted butter on top of cake. Bake for 10 more minutes or until done. Serve warm or cooled.

Yield: 1 (13 x 9 x 2-inch) coffee cake

Cinnamon-Nut Pound Cake

Great to serve with coffee at breakfast or brunch

1 cup butter or margarine, softened
2 cups sugar
2 large eggs
2 cups all-purpose flour
1¼ teaspoons baking powder
¼ teaspoon salt
1 (8-ounce) container sour cream
1 teaspoon vanilla extract
½ to 1 cup finely chopped pecans
1 teaspoon sugar
1 teaspoon ground cinnamon

▸ Grease and flour a 10-inch Bundt or tube pan.
▸ Beat butter at medium speed with an electric mixer 2 minutes or until creamy; gradually add 2 cups sugar, beating 5 to 7 minutes. Add eggs, 1 at a time, beating just until yellow disappears after each addition.
▸ Combine flour, baking powder, and salt; add to butter mixture alternately with sour cream, beginning and ending with flour mixture and beating at low speed just until blended after each addition. Stir in vanilla and nuts.
▸ Pour half of batter into prepared pan.
▸ Combine 1 teaspoon sugar and cinnamon; sprinkle over batter in pan. Top with remaining batter.
▸ Bake at 325° for 1 hour to 1 hour and 30 minutes or until a wooden pick inserted in cake comes out clean. Remove from oven and let cool on a wire rack 10 to 15 minutes.
▸ Remove cake from pan and let cool completely on wire rack.

Yield: 1 (10-inch) cake

Nutty Danish Pastry

Absolutely unbelievable!

2 cups all-purpose flour, divided
Dash of salt
½ cup butter, cut into ½-inch pieces and frozen
2 to 3 tablespoons water
1 cup water
½ cup butter
1 teaspoon almond extract
3 large eggs
⅔ cup finely chopped pecans
Cream Cheese Glaze

- Process 1 cup flour, salt, and frozen butter in a food processor until mixture resembles coarse meal. With machine running, add 2 to 3 tablespoons water, 1 tablespoon at a time, through food chute until mixture almost forms a ball.
- Form dough into a ball and divide into 2 portions; pat each portion into a 12 x 3-inch rectangle on an ungreased baking sheet.
- Bring 1 cup water and ½ cup butter to a boil in a saucepan, stirring constantly until butter is melted. Stir in remaining 1 cup flour and almond extract and reduce heat to low. Cook, stirring constantly, until mixture forms a ball of dough and leaves sides of pan. Remove from heat and let cool 5 minutes.
- Transfer dough to food processor. With machine running, add eggs through food chute, 1 at a time, processing until mixture is smooth and shiny after each addition. Spread half of mixture over each rectangle.
- Bake at 350° for 1 hour or until topping is crisp and browned.
- Spread Cream Cheese Glaze over hot pastry and sprinkle with nuts.

Yield: 6 to 8 servings

Cream Cheese Glaze
1 (3-ounce) package cream cheese, cubed and softened
2 cups sifted powdered sugar
1 teaspoon vanilla extract
1 to 2 tablespoons milk

- Process first 3 ingredients and 1 tablespoon milk in a food processor until well blended; add remaining milk, 1 teaspoon at a time, processing until smooth and desired consistency.

Yield: about 1 cup

Appetizers

The Blank Canvas

Art Exhibits

When visitors come to the Center for Cultural Arts to attend a meeting, purchase tickets to an event or grab lunch in the restaurant, they might miss the facility's most dramatic element.

In the Center's magnificent atrium is a pair of towering escalators. A trip to the top takes visitors to a trio of exhibition halls. Throughout the year, each hall features exhibits by national, regional and local artists.

The Main Exhibition Hall offers collections of sculpture, folk art, crafts, photography, canvas art, needle-art and more. Among past highlights have been paintings by world-renowned artists Howard Finster and Lowell Nesbitt. Important collections that have been presented include the *Faberge Silver from the Forbes Collection* and *Chinese Cloisonne from the Pierre Uldry Collection*. Special shows like the children's exhibit *Dinosaurs Alive*; a 50th anniversary commemoration, *Lest We Forget, Voices and Images of World War II* and the annual *Festival of Trees* have occupied the Main Hall.

In the Heritage Room, the Center's second largest exhibition hall, visitors can always find other striking works of art, everything from hand-tinted photography to metal sculpture.

The Center's third hall is known as the pARTnership Gallery. It features changing collections by local artists and is an important forum for artists to introduce their work.

Since opening in 1990, the Center has hosted more than 150 exhibits in its more than 6,500 square feet of exhibition space. With a track record of quality shows and the availability of expansive space, the Center enjoys a reputation among Southeastern artists as an outstanding place to display their works.

Muffuletta Phyllo Purses

A Cultural Arts League signature recipe

1 (12-ounce) jar pickled mixed vegetables, drained and coarsely chopped
1 cup Olive Salad (see page 97)
12 phyllo sheets
Butter-flavored cooking spray
2 ¼ cups finely shredded provolone cheese
Ground pepper
¼ pound hard Genoa salami, chopped into ½-inch pieces

▸ Combine mixed vegetables and Olive Salad in a bowl. Set aside.
▸ Place 1 phyllo sheet on wax paper; coat with butter-flavored cooking spray. Layer 2 more sheets on top, coating each with cooking spray. Cut layers into 9 rectangles using kitchen shears.
▸ Place 1 tablespoon of cheese in the center of each rectangle. Spoon 1 level tablespoon of vegetable mixture over cheese. Sprinkle lightly with pepper and top with salami.
▸ Gather corners of phyllo over filling to form a bundle and gently twist to close. Lightly coat with cooking spray and place on an ungreased baking sheet.
▸ Repeat procedure with remaining phyllo sheets, vegetable mixture, cheese, and salami.
▸ Bake at 350° for 12 to 15 minutes or until golden brown. Serve hot or at room temperature.

Yield: 3 dozen

NOTE: *To make in advance, assemble as directed above. Bake at 350° for 8 minutes or until lightly browned. Transfer to a container and cover tightly. Chill. When ready to serve, remove from refrigerator and let stand at room temperature 1 hour. Place on a baking sheet and bake at 350° for 5 to 10 minutes or until browned and thoroughly heated.*

Market Place Smoked Salmon

On a scale of 1 to 5, this is a 10! This distinctive smoked salmon combines the cured flavor of gravlax and the drier texture of wood-smoked fish.

1 (3- to 4-pound) salmon fillet with skin attached
1 tablespoon cognac
2 tablespoons sugar
1 tablespoon coarse-grained sea salt or Kosher salt
2 tablespoons fresh dill sprigs
3 shallots, finely sliced
Olive oil
2 cups hickory chips, soaked in water
Garnishes: fresh dill, lemon slices, lettuce, cucumber

▸ Remove pin bones from salmon fillet. Lightly moisten flesh side of salmon with cognac.
▸ Combine sugar, salt, and dill; sprinkle evenly over salmon. Place sliced shallots evenly over salmon.
▸ Place salmon in a 13 x 9 x 2-inch baking dish and cover with plastic wrap. Place a 12 x 8 x 2-inch pan or baking dish on top of salmon and arrange several unopened cans of food on their sides in the pan to weight the salmon down.
▸ Chill 24 hours to cure the salmon.
▸ Remove from refrigerator and brush the salmon skin with olive oil.
▸ Prepare smoker according to manufacturer's directions.
▸ Drain hickory chips and place on coals or as directed on package.
▸ Place water pan in smoker; fill at least ⅔ full and add skins from the shallots.
▸ Place salmon, skin side down, on well-oiled food rack; cover with smoker lid.
▸ Cook 1 hour or until fish flakes with a fork. Remove from smoker and let cool at room temperature.
▸ Serve immediately or chill until ready to serve.
▸ Serve salmon on toast points with lemon wedges, dill mayonnaise, horseradish sauce, capers, chopped onion, and cream cheese.
Yield: 24 to 36 appetizer servings

Nova Scotia Salmon Mold

Impress your guests with this beautiful and delicious salmon spread.

1 envelope unflavored gelatin
¼ cup cold water
½ cup whipping cream
1 (8-ounce) package cream cheese, softened
1 cup sour cream
1 teaspoon Worcestershire sauce
Dash of hot sauce
1 teaspoon fresh lemon juice
2 tablespoons green onions, finely chopped
1 tablespoon fresh parsley, finely chopped
1 tablespoon prepared horseradish
8 ounces Nova Scotia salmon, chopped
1 (4-ounce) jar red caviar, drained

▸ Sprinkle gelatin over ¼ cup cold water in a small saucepan; let stand 1 minute. Cook over low heat, stirring constantly, 2 minutes or until gelatin dissolves. Stir in whipping cream.

▸ Beat gelatin mixture and cream cheese at medium speed with an electric mixer 5 minutes or until mixture is smooth. Add sour cream, Worcestershire sauce, hot sauce, and lemon juice; beat at low speed 1 minute to blend.

▸ Fold in green onions, parsley, horseradish, and salmon. Gently fold in caviar. Pour into a lightly-greased 3-quart plastic or ceramic mold. Chill 3 hours or until firm.

▸ Unmold and serve.

Yield: 20 servings

Marinated Shrimp

This easy-to-prepare hors d'oeuvre is always a hit.

1 cup olive oil
½ cup white vinegar
2½ tablespoons capers and juice
1½ teaspoons salt
Dash of hot sauce
2½ pounds medium-size fresh shrimp, cooked, peeled, and deveined
2 cups thinly sliced onion
1 (14-ounce) can artichoke hearts, drained and quartered
1 (5.75-ounce) can pitted ripe olives, drained

▸ Combine first 5 ingredients in a bowl; add shrimp, onions, artichoke hearts and olives, tossing to coat.
▸ Cover and chill 2 hours.
Yield: 10 servings

Spicy Marinated Shrimp

Layers of shrimp, purple onion, and lemons make a colorful presentation.

2 pounds medium-size fresh shrimp, cooked, peeled and deveined
  (with tails left on)
1 large purple onion, sliced
2 large lemons, sliced
½ cup extra virgin olive oil
¼ cup white wine vinegar
2 tablespoons fresh lemon juice
1 garlic clove, halved
1 bay leaf, crumbled
1 teaspoon dry mustard
1 teaspoon dried basil, crumbled
1 teaspoon salt
⅛ teaspoon pepper
3 or 4 whole allspice
Garnish: fresh parsley sprigs

▸ Layer first 3 ingredients in a large covered container.
▸ Combine oil, vinegar, lemon juice, garlic, bay leaf, mustard, basil, salt, pepper, and allspice in a jar; cover tightly and shake vigorously.
▸ Pour marinade over shrimp mixture, tossing gently to coat. Cover and chill

8 hours or overnight, tossing occasionally.

▸ Serve with wooden picks and garnish, if desired.

Yield: 8 servings

NOTE: Marinade can be prepared the day before and chilled until poured over shrimp.

Goat Cheese Tarts

Bite-size savory cheesecakes for your next cocktail party.

Butter-flavored cooking spray
1 cup soft French breadcrumbs
3 tablespoons butter, melted
1 teaspoon salt, divided
1 teaspoon freshly ground pepper, divided
11 ounces cream cheese, softened
2 (3.5-ounce) packages goat cheese
2 large eggs, lightly beaten
2 tablespoons chopped fresh chives
½ cup diced red bell pepper
½ cup chopped walnut pieces

▸ Coat 5 miniature muffin pans with butter-flavored cooking spray.

▸ Combine breadcrumbs, butter, ½ teaspoon salt, and ½ teaspoon pepper in a bowl, stirring well. Spoon a heaping teaspoon into each miniature muffin pan cup, pressing into bottom.

▸ Beat cream cheese at medium speed with an electric mixer until light and fluffy; add goat cheese and beat until creamy. Add eggs, beating well. Stir in chives and remaining ½ teaspoon salt and ½ teaspoon pepper.

▸ Spoon mixture into muffin pans, filling three-fourths full. Top half with chopped red bell pepper and half with walnut pieces.

▸ Bake at 375° for 12 to 15 minutes or until puffy. Remove from oven and let cool on wire racks 5 minutes. Remove from pans, using a knife to loosen edges.

Yield: 5 dozen

NOTE: If you do not have enough miniature muffin pans, bake tarts in batches and reheat them in a 350° oven 5 minutes. To prepare ahead, pour filling into crusts; cover and chill until ready to bake. Remove from refrigerator and let stand at room temperature 15 minutes before baking.

Spinach Balls

Nice idea for a cocktail supper

2 (10-ounce) packages frozen chopped spinach
3 cups herb-seasoned stuffing mix
1½ cups finely chopped onion
6 large eggs, lightly beaten
½ teaspoon pepper
½ cup grated Parmesan cheese
1 tablespoon Accent
½ teaspoon thyme
¾ cup butter, melted

- ▸ Cook spinach according to package directions; drain well, pressing between layers of paper towels.
- ▸ Combine spinach and remaining ingredients in a large bowl, stirring well. Roll into small balls and place on baking sheets.
- ▸ Bake at 350° for 20 minutes.

Yield: about 100 balls

NOTE: *Spinach balls can be frozen before they are baked. When ready to serve, let thaw in refrigerator and bake as directed.*

Lite Ham-Stuffed New Potatoes

These are so good no one even cares that they are lower in fat.

15 small new potatoes, unpeeled
1 cup diced cooked ham
⅓ cup low-fat ricotta cheese
2 tablespoons Neufchâtel cheese
2 tablespoons nonfat cottage cheese
1 tablespoon minced onion
1 tablespoon Dijon mustard
Paprika

- ▸ Arrange potatoes in a steamer basket over boiling water; cover and steam 20 minutes or until tender. Remove from steamer and let cool.
- ▸ Scoop out center of potatoes with a melon baller, reserving potato pulp for another use.
- ▸ Combine ham, cheeses, onion, and mustard, stirring well. Spoon into potatoes and sprinkle with paprika.

Yield: 15 servings

Cucumber Sandwiches

A perennial favorite

1 (8-ounce) package cream cheese, softened
2 tablespoons mayonnaise
4 green onions, chopped (only the white part)
¼ teaspoon seasoned pepper
¼ teaspoon garlic salt
1 tablespoon lemon juice
1 European cucumber, peeled and scored with a fork
1 (about 30 slices) white or wheat loaf of bread

▸ Beat first 6 ingredients at medium speed with an electric mixer
until smooth.
▸ Cut cucumber into ⅛-inch slices and place on paper towels to drain.
▸ Using a small biscuit cutter, cut each bread slice into 3 or 4 (1⅛-inch)
rounds. Spread each round with 1 teaspoon cream cheese mixture and top
with a cucumber slice.
▸ Layer sandwiches in an airtight container. Separate layers with wax paper.
Cover and refrigerate.
Yield: about 75 sandwiches
NOTE: *To make ahead: Store sliced cucumbers and prepared rounds separately.*
Assemble when ready to serve.

Spiced Pecans

Great for cocktails or dessert buffet

1 egg white
¼ cup sugar
1 teaspoon ground cinnamon
Dash of salt
4 cups pecan halves

▸ Combine first 4 ingredients, stirring well. Pour over pecans, stirring to coat
well. Spread pecans in two ungreased jelly-roll pans.
▸ Bake at 300° for 30 minutes or until dry, stirring once. Remove from baking
sheet immediately.
Yield: 4 cups

Crunchy Munchy Pecans

The perfect accompaniment to Rick's Bloody Mary (see page 56).

½ cup butter
2 teaspoons Worcestershire sauce
1 teaspoon hot sauce
2 teaspoons garlic or seasoned salt
6 cups pecan halves

- Melt butter in a Dutch oven over medium heat. Remove from heat and add Worcestershire sauce, hot sauce, and salt, stirring well. Add pecans, stirring to coat. Spread pecans evenly on 2 (15 x 10-inch) jelly-roll pans.
- Bake at 350° for 13 to 15 minutes or until toasted, stirring every 5 minutes.
- Drain on brown paper until cool.

Yield: 6 cups

Easy Cheese Wafers

Very easy and very good. Use a pastry blender to evenly mark the slices before cutting with a knife.

½ cup butter or margarine, softened
2 cups (8 ounces) shredded sharp cheddar cheese, softened
1½ cups all-purpose flour
½ teaspoon salt
⅛ teaspoon ground red pepper
½ cup finely chopped pecans

- Beat margarine and cheese at medium speed with an electric mixer until creamy; add flour, salt, and red pepper, beating to blend. Stir in pecans.
- Roll dough into a log and wrap in plastic wrap. Chill 2 hours or until firm for easier slicing.
- Cut dough into ¼-inch slices and place on an ungreased baking sheet.
- Bake at 350° for 8 to 10 minutes or until lightly browned (do not over bake).

Yield: about 6 dozen

Crispy Cheese Wafers

Crispy rice cereal adds extra crunch.

2 cups all-purpose flour
2 cups (8 ounces) shredded sharp cheddar cheese, softened
1 cup butter or margarine, softened
1 teaspoon Worcestershire sauce
1 teaspoon salt
1 teaspoon ground red pepper
½ teaspoon paprika
1 cup chopped pecans (optional)
2 cups crisp rice cereal

▸ Beat first 7 ingredients at medium speed with an electric mixer until blended. Stir in pecans and rice cereal.
▸ Shape dough into 2 logs. Wrap in plastic wrap and chill thoroughly.
▸ Score logs with a pastry blender and slice. Place slices on ungreased baking sheets.
▸ Bake at 350° for 10 to 15 minutes or until lightly browned.
Yield: about 12 dozen

Cheese Straws

Nobody can eat just one!

2 cups (8 ounces) shredded sharp cheddar cheese, softened
4 cups (16 ounces) shredded extra-sharp cheddar cheese, softened
¾ cup corn oil margarine, softened
3 cups all-purpose flour
¾ teaspoon salt
¾ teaspoon ground red pepper

▸ Combine all ingredients in a large bowl, stirring until well blended.
▸ Following manufacturer's instructions, fit a cookie press with a star-shaped disk. Shape dough into long straws onto ungreased baking sheets.
▸ Bake at 350° for 15 minutes or until crisp. Remove from oven and let cool on wire racks.
▸ Break straws into shorter pieces and store in an airtight container.
Yield: 8 dozen

Pecan-Crusted Artichoke Cheese Spread

For ease of preparation, use bags of prewashed spinach. Place spinach in bowl and coarsely cut using kitchen shears.

3 tablespoons butter
½ cup diced onion
2 garlic cloves, minced
4 cups coarsely, chopped fresh spinach
1 (14-ounce) can artichoke hearts, drained and chopped
1 (8-ounce) package cream cheese, cut into pieces
½ cup mayonnaise
¾ cup shredded Parmesan cheese
1 cup (4 ounces) shredded Monterey Jack cheese
1 cup (4 ounces) shredded cheddar cheese
1 tablespoon butter, melted
⅔ cup chopped pecans
½ cup herb-seasoned stuffing mix
Pita Bread Triangles, French bread rounds, or crackers

▸ Melt 3 tablespoons butter in a large skillet over medium heat; add onion and garlic and sauté until tender. Add spinach and cook over medium heat, for 3 minutes, stirring often.
▸ Add artichoke hearts, cream cheese, mayonnaise, and cheeses; cook, stirring often, until cheese is melted. Spoon into a 2-quart baking dish.
▸ Bake at 350° for 20 minutes. Stir gently.
▸ Combine melted butter, pecans, and stuffing mix, tossing to blend. Sprinkle over top of dip. Bake 15 more minutes or until browned.
▸ Serve dip with Pita Bread Triangles.

Pita Bread Triangles

1 (12-ounce) package pita bread rounds

▸ Cut each round in half horizontally; cut each round into 8 wedges. Place wedges on an ungreased baking sheet.
▸ Bake at 350° for 15 to 20 minutes or until lightly browned. Remove from oven and let cool on wire racks.
Yield: 8 dozen triangles

Vidalia Onion Dip

Thank goodness sweet onions are available all year!

2 cups chopped sweet onion
1 cup (4 ounces) shredded sharp cheddar cheese
1 cup (4 ounces) shredded Swiss cheese
1 cup mayonnaise

▸ Combine all ingredients in a bowl, stirring well. Spoon into a 9-inch glass pie plate or quiche dish coated with vegetable cooking spray.
▸ Bake at 350° for 20 to 25 minutes or until thoroughly heated.
▸ Serve dip warm with crackers.
Yield: 4½ cups

Reuben Dip

Hearty dip for football season

1 (8-ounce) package cream cheese, cut into pieces and softened
½ cup sour cream
1 (8-ounce) can sauerkraut, drained and chopped
½ pound cooked lean corned beef, finely chopped
2 teaspoons finely chopped onion
1 tablespoon ketchup
2 teaspoons spicy brown mustard
1 cup (4 ounces) shredded Swiss cheese

▸ Combine all ingredients in a bowl, stirring well. Spoon into a 1½-quart baking dish.
▸ Bake, covered, at 375° for 30 minutes or until bubbly around edges. Uncover and bake 5 more minutes or until golden brown.
▸ Serve dip with rye crackers or cocktail rye bread.
Yield: 2 cups

Hot Lite Artichoke Dip

We all like this lower fat version better than the original.

2 (14-ounce) cans artichoke hearts, drained and finely chopped
½ cup mayonnaise
½ cup plain nonfat yogurt
1 cup freshly grated Parmesan cheese
½ teaspoon garlic powder (optional)
Paprika

▸ Combine first 4 ingredients and, if desired, garlic powder, stirring gently. Spoon into a 1-quart baking dish coated with vegetable cooking spray. Sprinkle with paprika.
▸ Bake at 350° for 30 minutes or until thoroughly heated.
▸ Serve dip with Pita Bread Triangles (see page 44) or crackers.
Yield: about 3 cups

Bleu Cheese Mousse

A cocktail party favorite

2 envelopes unflavored gelatin
¼ cup cold water
1½ cups sour cream
½ cup chopped green onions
1 (1.6-ounce) envelope Italian dressing mix
1 cup bleu cheese, crumbled
2 cups small-curd cottage cheese
Garnish: cherry tomatoes

▸ Grease a 4-cup mold.
▸ Sprinkle gelatin over ¼ cup cold water in a 1-quart saucepan; let stand 5 minutes. Cook over medium heat, stirring constantly, until gelatin is dissolved.
▸ Process gelatin, sour cream, green onions, dressing mix, bleu cheese, and cottage cheese in a food processor until smooth. Pour into prepared mold and cover with plastic wrap. Cover and chill until firm.
▸ When ready to serve, unmold onto a serving platter by running a knife tip around the edges and dipping the bottom of the mold into warm water for 1 minute.
▸ When ready to serve, unmold onto a lettuce lined plate. Garnish if desired.
Yield: 8 to 10 servings

Baja Spinach Dip

Take care of last minute party details while this is in the oven.

1 medium onion, chopped
2 tablespoons vegetable oil
2 tomatoes, chopped
2 tablespoons canned chopped green chiles
1 (10-ounce) package frozen chopped spinach, thawed, well drained
2 cups shredded Monterey Jack cheese
1 (8-ounce) package cream cheese, cut into chunks, softened
1 cup half-and-half
2 (3-ounce) cans sliced black olives, drained
1 tablespoon red wine vinegar
Salt and pepper to taste
Hot pepper sauce to taste

▸ Sauté onion in oil in large skillet until tender. Stir in tomatoes and green chiles.
▸ In a large mixing bowl, combine onion mixture with spinach, Monterey Jack cheese, cream cheese, half-and-half, olives and wine vinegar. Mix well. Season with salt, pepper and hot pepper.
▸ Spoon mixture into a 9 x 12-inch glass baking dish. Bake at 350° for 30 minutes or until bubbly.
▸ Serve with tortilla chips.
Yield: 12 servings

Joy's Cheddar Bleu

A recipe loved almost as much as the lady for whom it is named.

2 cups (8 ounces) shredded sharp cheddar cheese, softened
1 cup bleu cheese, crumbled
1 (8-ounce) package cream cheese, softened
1 tablespoon Worcestershire sauce
1 tablespoon chili sauce
1 tablespoon grated onion
½ cup chopped pecans

▸ Combine first 3 ingredients in a bowl, stirring well; add Worcestershire
  sauce, chili sauce, and onion, stirring well.
▸ Shape mixture into a 6-inch ball and roll in chopped pecans until evenly
  coated. Wrap in plastic wrap and chill.
▸ Serve cheese ball with assorted crackers.
Yield: 1 (6-inch) cheese ball

Creamy Cheddar with Apricot Chutney

In a hurry? Top this cheese mixture with a jar of your favorite chutney.

1 (6-ounce) package dried apricots, finely chopped
¾ cup pineapple juice
½ cup dried cranberries or raisins
¼ cup chutney
¼ cup brandy
2 cups (8 ounces) shredded mild cheddar cheese, softened
2 (8-ounce) packages cream cheese, cubed and softened

▸ Bring first 5 ingredients to a boil in a small saucepan over medium heat;
  boil, stirring often, 8 to 10 minutes or until most of liquid is evaporated.
  Remove from heat and let cool completely. Chill.
▸ Line a 3-cup mold with plastic wrap.
▸ Process cheeses in a food processor until smooth; pack mixture into
  prepared mold. Cover and chill 12 hours.
▸ Invert cheese onto a serving platter, removing plastic wrap. Spoon apricot
  mixture over top. Serve with apple or pear slices and gingersnaps.
Yield: 2⅔ cups

Gouda Cheese Spread

Creamy texture and nice flavor

1 (8-ounce) Gouda cheese round
½ cup sour cream
1½ teaspoons Italian salad dressing mix

▶ Cut circle from top of gouda. Hollow out, leaving about ¼-inch cheese on all sides.
▶ Cut Gouda in ½-inch pieces.
▶ Combine cheese, sour cream, and dressing mix in small mixer bowl; beat until smooth. Spoon into cheese shell. Chill.
▶ Serve cheese spread with assorted crackers.

Yield: 1¼ cups
NOTE: *One (8-ounce) wedge of Gouda cheese may be substituted for round. Serve in bowl.*

Peppercorn Cheese

Men love this cheese. Coarsely cracked fresh peppercorns deliver more flavor than ground pepper.

2 (8-ounce) packages cream cheese, softened
4 green onions, finely chopped
1 tablespoon Worcestershire sauce
1 shallot, finely chopped
1 tablespoon black peppercorns, coarsely cracked
1 tablespoon pink peppercorns, coarsely cracked
1 tablespoon white peppercorns, coarsely cracked

▶ Combine first 4 ingredients in a bowl, stirring to blend. Divide mixture into thirds and place each portion on a sheet of wax paper. Chill until slightly firm.
▶ Shape each portion into a 6-inch log about 1½ to 2 inches in diameter.
▶ Combine cracked peppercorns; roll each cheese log in mixture, coating evenly. Wrap in heavy-duty plastic wrap and chill until firm.
▶ Serve cheese logs with assorted crackers.

Yield: 3 (2-inch) logs

Sun-Dried Tomato Cheese

An interesting blend for discriminating tastes

1 (7- or 8-ounce) jar sun-dried tomatoes packed in oil
1 garlic clove, halved
2 teaspoons dried basil
3 (8-ounce) packages cream cheese, softened
¾ cup chopped fresh parsley or toasted chopped walnuts

▸ Drain tomatoes, reserving oil for another use.
▸ Process tomatoes and 1 garlic clove in a food processor until finely chopped; add basil and cream cheese and process just until blended. Chill until slightly firm.
▸ Shape cheese mixture into a ball and flatten into a 2-inch thick round. Dip in parsley or walnuts to coat, pressing lightly into cheese.
▸ Serve cheese round with crackers, Melba toast, or toasted French bread.
Yield: 1 cheese round

Easy Cheezy Bleu

Easy, easy, easy! No shredding, just mix!

11 ounces cream cheese, softened
1 (5-ounce) jar Old English cheese spread
4 ounces bleu cheese
3 tablespoons chopped onion
2 tablespoons chopped fresh parsley
½ teaspoon garlic powder
1 cup finely chopped pecans, divided

▸ Beat first 6 ingredients and ½ cup pecans at medium speed with an electric mixer until well blended. Cover and chill until slightly firm.
▸ Shape cheese mixture into a ball and roll in remaining ½ cup pecans. Chill.
▸ Serve with your choice of crackers.
Yield: 1 cheese ball

Boursin Cheese

A lightly seasoned buttery cheese that's wonderful with dry white and fruity red wines

1 garlic clove, minced
⅛ teaspoon ground thyme
2 tablespoons finely chopped fresh parsley
1 tablespoon chopped fresh chives
1 (8-ounce) package cream cheese, softened
3 tablespoons butter or margarine, softened
Freshly ground pepper or minced fresh parsley

▸ Combine first 4 ingredients in a bowl, stirring with a wooden spoon; add cream cheese and butter, stirring until well blended.
▸ Shape cheese mixture into a ball and sprinkle lightly with pepper or parsley until coated. Cover and chill thoroughly.
Yield: 8 to 10 servings

Amaretto Brie

A sweet cheese and pretty presentation for a dessert buffet

1 (2-pound) Brie cheese round
1½ cups chopped pecans
¼ cup firmly packed brown sugar
¼ cup amaretto

▸ Cut rind from top of Brie leaving a 1-inch border around the top.
▸ Combine pecans, brown sugar, and amaretto, stirring well. Spread over top of Brie.
▸ Broil 8 inches from heat 2 to 5 minutes or until cheese is slightly softened.
▸ Serve with gingersnaps, crackers, and pear and apple slices.
Yield: 1 (2-pound) round

Evelyne S. Terrell's Tea

A delicious and easy tea. It's great for a crowd and can be made a day ahead.

2 quarts water, divided
2 family-size flow-through tea bags
1½ to 2 cups sugar
1 (6-ounce) can frozen lemonade concentrate, thawed and undiluted

▸ Bring 1 quart water to a boil in a saucepan; remove from heat and add tea bags. Let steep 30 to 45 minutes.
▸ Pour remaining 1 quart water into a 1-gallon jug; add sugar, lemonade concentrate, and tea. Stir well and fill to top with water. Chill.
Yield: 1 gallon

Delta Mint Tea

Southerners keep it in the refrigerator all year round.

7 lemons, divided
7 regular-size tea bags
12 fresh mint sprigs
8 cups boiling water
2 cups sugar
8 cups water

▸ Grate the rind of 3 lemons, reserving lemons.
▸ Combine lemon rind, tea bags, mint sprigs, and 8 cups boiling water; let steep 12 minutes. Remove and discard tea bags; pour tea into a 1-gallon container through a wire-mesh strainer, discarding mint and lemon rind.
▸ Juice 7 lemons. Add lemon juice to tea. Add sugar, stirring to dissolve.
▸ Add 8 cups water, stirring well. Chill.
Yield: 1 gallon

Cottage Punch

Delicious!

1 (46-ounce) bottle unsweetened apple juice, chilled
1 (46-ounce) can unsweetened pineapple juice, chilled
1 (6-ounce) can frozen lemonade concentrate, thawed and undiluted
1 (1-litre) bottle ginger ale, chilled

▸ Combine first 3 ingredients in a large punch bowl; stir in ginger ale.
Yield: 1 gallon

Fruit Smoothies

Freezing the fruit makes these "health shakes" thicker without adding ice.

1 cup fresh strawberries, cut into halves
1 large banana, cut into 1-inch thick slices
¼ cup apple, apple-grape, cranberry, or orange juice
1 cup low-fat milk
1 cup plain yogurt or ¼ cup soft tofu

▸ Place berries and banana slices on a paper plate; freeze until firm.
▸ Place frozen berries, frozen banana, juice, milk, and yogurt in a blender;
place cover on top and process until smooth, stopping to scrape
down sides.
Yield: 3 cups
NOTE: Any variety of fresh, frozen, or canned fruit may be substituted.

Sparkling Sangría

Bubbly beverages rather than wine add fizz to this refreshing "mocktail."
Great for brunch or cocktails

1 (750 ml) bottle white sparkling grape juice, chilled
3 cups cranberry-apple juice, chilled
1 cup fresh orange juice, chilled
1 (10-ounce) bottle sparkling water, chilled
1 orange
1 lime

▸ Combine first 4 ingredients in a large pitcher.
▸ Slice the orange and the lime and cut each slice in half; add fruit to sangría,
stirring well. Serve over ice.
Yield: 10 cups

Punch for a Crowd

You can't make too much of this refreshing drink.

1 (0.23-ounce) envelope lemon-flavored unsweetened drink mix
1 quart water
1 (12-ounce) can frozen orange juice concentrate, thawed and undiluted
1 (6-ounce) can frozen lemonade concentrate, thawed and undiluted
1 (46-ounce) can pineapple juice
1 (2-liter) bottle ginger ale, chilled

▸ Combine drink mix and 1 quart water in a gallon container, stirring well. Add orange and lemonade concentrates, pineapple juice, and enough water to make 1 gallon, stirring well.
▸ Pour mixture into 2 (½-gallon) juice cartons.
▸ Freeze at least 8 hours, shaking the cartons twice.
▸ When ready to serve, remove from freezer and let stand at room temperature 4 to 5 hours or until slushy. Cut top off juice cartons and pour slushy mixture into punch bowl.
▸ Add ginger ale and stir.
Yield: 6 quarts

Holiday Hot Punch

The spicy aroma announces the season.

1½ cups apricot nectar
4 cups unsweetened pineapple juice
2 cups apple cider or juice
1 cup orange juice
1 (6-inch) cinnamon stick, broken into pieces
1 teaspoon whole cloves
4 whole cardamom, broken apart with husks discarded, or ½ teaspoon ground cardamom
White rum (optional)

▸ Bring first 7 ingredients to a boil in a Dutch oven over medium-high heat. Reduce heat and simmer 15 to 20 minutes.
▸ Pour punch through a wire-mesh strainer, discarding solids. Serve hot.
▸ Add a splash of rum to each cup, if desired.
Yield: about ½ gallon

League Punch

We are almost embarrassed to publish our secret. It's so easy and so refreshing.

1 (64-ounce) bottle white grape juice, chilled
1 (2-liter) ginger ale, chilled
Garnish: ice ring, sliced lemons, limes or oranges

▸ Combine grape juice and ginger ale in a punch bowl, stirring gently.
  Garnish, if desired.
Yield: about 1 gallon

Mint Juleps by the Pitcher

An easy way to serve juleps for a crowd. Take a sip, close your eyes,
and step back in time.

Mint Syrup
1½ cups coarsely chopped fresh mint
2 cups sugar
2 cups water

▸ Tie mint in a cheesecloth bag; place in a 2-quart saucepan.
▸ Add sugar and 2 cups water to saucepan and bring to a boil. Cook,
  stirring constantly, until sugar dissolves. Remove from heat and let stand
  4 to 6 hours.
▸ Remove and discard cheesecloth bag.
Yield: about 2 cups

Juleps
6 cups bourbon
1½ cups Mint Syrup
Crushed ice
Garnish: fresh mint sprigs

▸ Combine bourbon and Mint Syrup in a large pitcher.
▸ Place ice in a large punch bowl. Place wine glasses or julep cups,
  rim side down, in ice.
▸ Spoon ice into chilled glasses and add enough bourbon mixture to just
  cover ice; stir gently and garnish, if desired.
Yield: 24 servings
NOTE: *For individual servings, combine ¼ cup bourbon and 1 tablespoon Mint Syrup.*

Whiskey Sour Punch

This was a smashing success at our '99 Auction.

1 (12-ounce) can frozen lemonade concentrate, thawed and undiluted
1½ cups whiskey
1 (2-litre) bottle ginger ale, chilled
1½ cups water, chilled
Garnish: ice ring with cherries with stems, orange slices, lemon slices, and pineapple slices

▸ Combine first 4 ingredients in a pitcher or a punch bowl, stirring well. Garnish, if desired.

Yield: 9 cups

Rick's Bloody Mary

Hot and spicy wake-up call.

6 cups tomato-based vegetable juice
4 cloves garlic, minced and mashed
1 teaspoon hot sauce
½ to 1 teaspoon seasoned salt
¼ to ½ teaspoon celery salt
¾ teaspoon black pepper
3 to 4 tablespoons prepared horseradish
3 to 4 tablespoons Worcestershire sauce
2 tablespoons beef bouillon granules
2 tablespoons hot water
Juice of 1 lemon
1½ cups vodka
Garnish: celery stalks

▸ Combine vegetable juice and next 7 ingredients in a large pitcher.
▸ Dissolve bouillon granules in hot water and add to vegetable juice.
▸ Juice one lemon. Add juice and lemon halves to vegetable juice. Stir well. Chill until ready to serve.
▸ Stir in vodka just before serving. Serve over ice and garnish if desired.

Yield: about 8 cups

Serendipity Sip

The Serendipity Dance Club served this festive drink at their Center Courtyard celebration.

4 cups gin
2 cups cherry brandy
¾ cup orange juice
¾ cup pineapple juice
½ cup lime juice or lemon juice
12 drops of Cointreau and Benedictine
4 dashes Angostura bitters
Garnish: cherries and pineapple slices

▸ Combine all ingredients in a large pitcher. Stir well.
▸ Chill until ready to serve.
▸ Serve over ice and garnish if desired.
Yield: about 8 cups

Red Wine Sangría

Serve this refreshing fruit and red wine cooler with Creamy Chicken Enchiladas (see page 117).

1 cup orange juice, chilled
½ cup lemon juice, chilled
1 lemon or lime, sliced
2 oranges, sliced
1 (750 ml) bottle red wine, chilled
2 tablespoons brandy
¼ cup superfine sugar (optional)
1 (10-ounce) bottle chilled seltzer (optional)

▸ Combine first 6 ingredients in a large pitcher, stirring well. Cover and chill 4 hours.
▸ To serve add sugar, if desired. If you like it lighter and a little fizzy, add a splash of seltzer. Serve over ice.
Yield: about 8 cups

Easy White Wine Sangría

It's our favorite beverage for courtyard parties. And it's easy to make for a crowd.

1 (25.4-ounce) bottle Riesling or Chablis, chilled
1 (6-ounce) can frozen lemonade concentrate, thawed and undiluted
1 (10-ounce) bottle club soda, chilled
1 lime, thinly sliced
1 lemon, thinly sliced
1 medium orange, thinly sliced

▸ Combine wine and lemonade in a pitcher, stirring well. Gently stir in club soda and fruit. Serve over ice.

Yield: 5 cups

Plantation Coffee Punch

Great for an after dinner drink or dessert buffet.

⅓ cup instant coffee granules
1 cup milk, heated
¼ cup sugar
Dash of salt
4 cups milk, chilled
1 teaspoon vanilla extract
½ cup coffee liqueur (optional)
1 pint vanilla or coffee ice cream, softened
1 pint whipping cream, whipped
Garnishes: dash of ground nutmeg or chocolate shavings

▸ Combine coffee granules and 1 cup heated milk in a pitcher, stirring until coffee is dissolved. Add sugar, salt, 4 cups chilled milk, vanilla, and, if desired, coffee liqueur, stirring well. Chill.
▸ Place softened ice cream in a punch bowl; pour coffee mixture over ice cream. Spoon whipped cream over punch. Garnish, if desired.

Yield: about 10 cups

Salads

First Position

Gadsden Community School for the Arts

Tell me, and I will forget,
Show me, and I will remember,
Involve me, and I will understand.
-Chinese Proverb

As traditional classrooms empty in the afternoon, the studios at the Gadsden Community School for the Arts come alive. Each week, hundreds of students, from preschoolers to adults, study with the GCSA's talented instructors. They learn ballet, jazz, watercolor, photography, drawing, voice, piano, violin and much more. Whether students participate in their first ballet class or pursue a career as a professional violinist, they all benefit from adding creative expression to their lives.

As one of only four Alabama art schools certified by the National Guild of Community Schools for the Arts, the GCSA offers affordable instruction as a supplement to the limited arts programs most students receive in school. In order to give opportunities to children who could benefit the most from exposure to the Arts, the GCSA is committed to providing scholarships.

The recitals and exhibits recognizing the GCSA students draw large, enthusiastic crowds. These events are a treat for family and visitors alike, and give students the positive reinforcement they need to continue their studies.

It is important for the Center for Cultural Arts to "tell" the community about the power of art, and to "show" them how beautiful it can be. But perhaps most important, the Center provides young and old a way in which to be "involved" in the Arts.

Sugared Almond Salad *with* Orange Vinaigrette

A springtime hit when strawberries are in season

Orange Vinaigrette
¾ cup extra-virgin olive oil
¼ cup red wine vinegar
1 teaspoon grated orange rind
1 tablespoon fresh orange juice
½ teaspoon poppy seeds
½ teaspoon salt
⅛ teaspoon pepper
Dash of hot sauce

▶ Combine all ingredients in a jar; cover tightly and shake vigorously. Store in refrigerator. Shake before each use.
Yield: 1 cup

Sugared Almond Salad
1 egg white
¼ cup sugar
1 cup sliced almonds
2 tablespoons butter or margarine, melted
1 head Bibb lettuce, torn into bite-size pieces
1 head leaf lettuce, torn into bite-size pieces
1 (11-ounce) can Mandarin orange sections, drained
1 pint strawberries, halved or quartered
2 green onions, chopped
Garnish: fresh whole strawberries

▶ Beat egg white at high speed with an electric mixer until foamy; gradually add sugar, 1 tablespoon at a time, beating until stiff peaks form. Fold in almonds.
▶ Pour butter into a 9-inch square pan. Spread coated almonds over butter.
▶ Bake at 325° for 20 to 25 minutes or until almonds are dry, stirring every 5 minutes. Remove from oven and let cool completely.
▶ Toss lettuce, orange sections, strawberries, and green onions in a bowl; add desired amount of Orange Vinaigrette and toss gently. Arrange salad on individual salad plates and sprinkle each serving with sugared almonds.
▶ Garnish, if desired.
Yield: 6 servings

Easy, Eggless Caesar Salad

No need for fancy table side presentation, simply shake the dressing in a jar.

Eggless Caesar Dressing
2 garlic cloves, minced
1 to 4 anchovy fillets, minced, or anchovy paste to taste
½ to 1 teaspoon salt
½ to 1 teaspoon freshly ground black pepper
2 tablespoons fresh lemon juice
2 teaspoons Worcestershire sauce
½ teaspoon Dijon mustard
2 tablespoons mayonnaise
½ cup extra-virgin olive oil

▶ Combine all ingredients in a jar; cover tightly and shake vigorously.
  Store in refrigerator up to 4 days. Shake before each use.
Yield: ⅔ cup

Caesar Salad
2 tablespoons butter, melted
2 tablespoons extra-virgin olive oil
1 (8 to 10-ounce) loaf rustic Italian bread
½ to 1 teaspoon salt
½ teaspoon freshly ground black pepper
⅛ teaspoon ground red pepper
2 (10-ounce) heads romaine lettuce, torn into 1 to 1½-inch pieces
3 to 6 ounces fresh Parmesan or Romano cheese, shaved with a
  vegetable peeler

▶ Combine butter and oil in a large bowl.
▶ Remove crusts from bread and cut bread into ½ to ¾-inch cubes.
  Add to butter and oil and toss to coat. Sprinkle with salt, black pepper,
  and red pepper and toss to coat. Spread in a single layer on a 15 x 10-inch
  jelly-roll pan.
▶ Bake at 450° for 10 to 12 minutes or until golden brown, stirring twice.
  Set aside.
▶ Place romaine in a large salad bowl and add desired amount of Eggless
  Caesar Dressing; toss to coat. Add croutons and cheese and toss well.
  Serve immediately.
Yield: 6 servings

Orange and Avocado Salad

A ripe avocado should yield to gentle palm pressure. To speed the ripening process, place in a brown paper bag and set aside at room temperature for 1 to 3 days. Store ripe avocado in refrigerator for several days.

Orange Dressing

½ cup fresh orange juice
¼ cup orange marmalade
2 tablespoons extra-virgin olive oil
1 tablespoon white vinegar
2 garlic cloves, minced
½ teaspoon salt
¼ teaspoon pepper

▸ Combine all ingredients in a jar; cover tightly and shake vigorously. Store in refrigerator. Shake before each use.

Yield: 1 cup

Avocado Salad

2 navel oranges
1 head red leaf lettuce, torn
1 small purple onion, thinly sliced
1 avocado, peeled and sliced

▸ Peel and section oranges.
▸ Place lettuce on 4 to 6 individual salad plates; arrange onion slices, orange sections, and avocado slices evenly on lettuce. Drizzle with desired amount of Orange Dressing.

Yield: 4 to 6 servings

Pear-Spinach Salad

A sweet and tangy combination of fruits and greens topped with crisp bacon

Pear-Spinach Salad
1 (29-ounce) can sliced pears in light syrup
1 pound loose fresh baby spinach
1 grapefruit, peeled and sectioned
½ cup thinly sliced green onions
3 slices bacon, cooked and crumbled

▸ Drain pears, reserving syrup for Lime-Parsley Dressing.
▸ Remove stems from spinach; wash thoroughly and pat dry. Tear into bite-size pieces.
▸ Combine spinach, grapefruit, and green onions in a large, shallow salad bowl. Add desired amount of Lime-Parsley Dressing and toss gently.
▸ Arrange pears on top and sprinkle with bacon.
Yield: 6 servings

Lime-Parsley Dressing
¼ cup reserved pear syrup
¼ cup vegetable oil
¼ cup red wine vinegar
1 tablespoon chopped fresh parsley
1 tablespoon lime juice
½ teaspoon salt
Dash of ground red pepper

▸ Combine all ingredients in a jar; cover tightly and shake vigorously. Store in refrigerator. Shake before each use.
Yield: ¾ cup

Autumn Dinner Salad

Sugar-glazed walnuts, pungent bleu cheese, and a tangy balsamic dressing lend an elegant flair.

Balsamic Vinaigrette
¾ cup extra-virgin olive oil
3 tablespoons balsamic vinegar
1 garlic clove, halved
1 teaspoon dry mustard

½ teaspoon seasoned salt
½ teaspoon onion juice
¼ teaspoon freshly ground pepper

▸ Combine all ingredients in a jar; cover tightly and shake vigorously. Let stand 1 hour. Remove and discard garlic. Store in refrigerator. Shake before each use.

Yield: about 1 cup

Autumn Dinner Salad

2 tablespoons butter
½ cup walnut halves
3 tablespoons brown sugar
6 cups mixed salad greens (romaine lettuce, leaf lettuce, Boston lettuce, radicchio), torn into bite-size pieces
3 green onions, chopped
1 firm pear or apple, thinly sliced
3 to 4 ounces crumbled bleu cheese

▸ Melt butter in a heavy skillet over medium heat; add walnuts and brown sugar and saute 6 to 7 minutes or until nuts begin to soften. Remove from pan to cool.
▸ Toss lettuce and green onions with desired amount of Balsamic Vinaigrette; arrange on individual salad plates. Arrange pear slices in a spiral over lettuce. Top with sugared nuts and bleu cheese. Serve immediately.

Yield: 4 servings

Marinated Broccoli Salad

"Great, and I don't even like raw broccoli."

1 bunch fresh broccoli, chopped
1 medium-size purple onion, diced
1 (8-ounce) bottle Italian dressing
1 or 2 tomatoes, diced
1 cup (4 ounces) shredded cheddar cheese

▸ Combine broccoli and onion in a medium serving dish; pour desired amount of Italian dressing over top and toss gently to coat. Cover and chill several hours or overnight.
▸ To serve, fold tomato and cheese into salad. Serve with a slotted spoon.

Yield: 6 to 8 servings

Buffet Spinach Salad
with Raspberry-Maple Dressing

Tailor this salad to your palate.

Raspberry-Maple Dressing
¼ cup maple syrup
½ cup raspberry vinegar
1 cup vegetable oil

▸ Combine all ingredients in a jar; cover tightly and shake vigorously. Store in refrigerator. Shake before each use.

Yield: 1¾ cup

Buffet Spinach Salad
1 (2.25-ounce) package sliced almonds
1 pound loose fresh baby spinach
1 pint strawberries, halved
1 (14-ounce) can Mandarin orange sections, drained
1 cup thinly sliced green onions
1 cup dried cranberries
1 cup raisins

▸ Bake almonds in a shallow pan at 350°, stirring occasionally, 5 to 10 minutes or until toasted.
▸ Remove stems from spinach; wash thoroughly and pat dry. Tear into bite-size pieces; chill until ready to serve.
▸ Place strawberries, orange sections, green onions, cranberries, raisins, and toasted almonds in small serving bowls.
▸ Pour Raspberry-Maple Dressing into a small pitcher or cruet.
▸ Place spinach in a large bowl and serve salad buffet-style with a choice of toppings.

Yield: 6 servings

Broccoli-Cauliflower Salad

Select broccoli that is deep green or green with a hint of purple. The buds should be tightly closed and the leaves crisp.

1 bunch broccoli, chopped
½ head cauliflower, chopped
½ cup chopped green olives
½ cup chopped onion
2 hard-cooked eggs, finely chopped
1 cup mayonnaise
2 teaspoons sugar
1 tablespoon lemon juice

▸ Combine first 5 ingredients in a large bowl.
▸ Combine mayonnaise, sugar, and lemon juice, stirring well. Add desired amount of mayonnaise mixture to salad, tossing to coat. Chill 2 hours before serving.
Yield: 8 servings

Cottage Cheese-Sour Cream Garden Salad

Serve in a tomato cup or as a spread with crackers.

1 cup sour cream
2 cups cream-style cottage cheese
¾ cup diced cucumber
½ cup sliced radishes
½ cup sliced green onions
¾ teaspoon salt
Garlic powder to taste
Pepper to taste

▸ Combine sour cream and cottage cheese in a medium-size bowl, blending well. Stir in cucumber, radishes, green onions, salt, garlic powder, and pepper. Chill 2 hours before serving.
Yield: 6 servings

Panzanella

This tomato and bread salad is an Italian speciality. It's a delicious way to savor summer tomatoes.

Fresh Basil Dressing
½ cup chopped fresh basil
½ cup extra-virgin olive oil
3 tablespoons balsamic or red wine vinegar
1 clove garlic, minced
½ teaspoon salt
½ teaspoon pepper

▸ Combine all ingredients in a jar; cover tightly and shake vigorously. Store in refrigerator. Shake before each use.

Yield: about ¾ cup

Bread Salad
4 cups cubed Italian bread
2 to 4 tablespoons extra-virgin olive oil
2 cups diced tomato
1 cup cubed cucumber, optional
¼ cup chopped red onion
¼ cup niçoise or kalamata olives
½ cup feta cheese

▸ Combine olive oil and bread cubes in a salad bowl, toss until evenly coated.
▸ Spread bread in a single layer on 15 x 10-inch jelly-roll pan. Bake at 375° until lightly toasted, about 5 to 8 minutes, stirring occasionally. Set aside.
▸ In salad bowl, combine toasted bread, tomato, cucumber, red onion, olives, garnish and desired amount of Fresh Basil Dressing.

OPTION: For Bean and Bread Salad, add 1 (15-ounce) can of chick peas or Great Northern beans, drained and rinsed.

Yield: 8 servings

Tomato, Caper, Olive, and Bleu Cheese Salad

Slices of juicy tomato are topped with a heady combination of flavorful ingredients in this robust side dish.

6 medium tomatoes, sliced
2 tablespoons balsamic vinegar
5 tablespoons olive oil
Salt and pepper
⅓ cup halved pitted kalamata olives
⅓ cup crumbled bleu cheese or feta cheese (about 2 ounces)
2 tablespoons drained capers
4 anchovies, drained and chopped (optional)
Garnish: fresh basil leaves

▸ Arrange tomato slices on a large serving platter.
▸ Combine vinegar and oil and drizzle over tomato slices; sprinkle very lightly with salt and generously with pepper.
▸ Top with olives, cheese, capers, and, if desired, chopped anchovy. Garnish, if desired.

Yield: 6 servings

Ruth's Potato Salad

This method of cooking the potatoes is the secret to a good potato salad.

2 pounds small red potatoes, unpeeled
4 hard-cooked eggs, coarsely chopped
½ cup finely chopped celery
½ cup chopped green or red bell pepper
1 to 1½ cups mayonnaise
2 tablespoons finely chopped onion (optional)
2 tablespoons sweet pickle relish (optional)
Salt and pepper to taste

▸ Cook potatoes in a Dutch oven in boiling salted water to cover 20 to 30 minutes or just until tender when pierced with a fork. Drain well.
▸ Cut a slit in each potato and return to Dutch oven without water. Cover and cook over low heat 2 to 3 minutes. Remove from heat and let stand, covered, until cool to touch. Peel and cube potatoes.
▸ Combine cubed potato, chopped egg, celery, bell pepper, mayonnaise, and, if desired, onion and relish; stir well. Add salt and pepper to taste.

Yield: 6 to 8 servings

Seafood Primavera with Basil Cream Sauce

A perfect spring and summer luncheon entrée that you can prepare a day ahead and assemble before serving.

Sherry Vinaigrette
½ cup white wine vinegar
3 tablespoons dry sherry
2 garlic cloves, crushed
1 teaspoon salt
⅔ cup olive oil

▸ Combine first 4 ingredients in a jar. Cover tightly and shake vigorously.
▸ Add oil and shake again.
Yield: 1½ cups

Basil Cream
6 tablespoons white wine vinegar
2 tablespoons Dijon mustard
⅔ cup fresh basil
2 garlic cloves
⅓ cup olive oil
1 cup sour cream
½ cup heavy cream
½ cup chopped fresh parsley
Salt and pepper to taste

▸ Process first 4 ingredients in a food processor until smooth. With machine running, add oil through food chute in a slow, steady stream to thicken (or emulsify).
▸ Add sour cream, cream, and parsley and puree until smooth.
▸ Season with salt and pepper to taste. Cover and chill.
Yield: 2⅔ cups

Seafood Primavera
8 ounces bowtie pasta
Salt and pepper to taste
2 pounds medium-size fresh shrimp, cooked, peeled, and deveined
1½ cups fresh broccoli florets
1½ cups frozen tiny green peas, thawed
4 carrots, cut into thin strips
16 fresh asparagus spears, cut into 1½-inch pieces
Romaine lettuce leaves
3 green onions, sliced diagonally
Garnish: fresh basil and 1 cup cherry tomatoes, cut into halves

- Cook pasta according to package directions; drain and rinse in cool water. Drain again.
- Toss together pasta and about ¼ cup Sherry Vinaigrette in a large bowl, reserving remaining vinaigrette; season with salt and pepper to taste. Cover and chill.
- Toss together shrimp and about ¼ cup Sherry Vinaigrette in a separate bowl; cover and chill.
- Blanch each vegetable (broccoli, carrots, asparagus) in boiling water for 2 to 3 minutes or until crisp tender; remove with a slotted spoon and plunge into cold water to stop cooking process; drain. Combine blanched vegetables with peas. Cover and chill.
- To serve, arrange lettuce leaves around the outer edge of a large serving platter.
- Toss together pasta, cooked vegetables, green onions, and about ¼ cup Basil Cream. Arrange on platter making a well in the center for the shrimp; fill center with shrimp. Garnish, if desired, and serve with remaining Basil Cream and Sherry Vinaigrette.

Yield: 6 to 8 servings

Black-Eyed Pea and Pasta Salad

Try this zesty Jalapeño Dressing on coleslaw, too.

Jalapeño Dressing
½ cup vegetable oil
2 tablespoons white wine vinegar
1 teaspoon sugar
1 teaspoon salt
1 teaspoon dry mustard
2 jalapeño peppers, seeded and finely chopped (about 2 tablespoons)
⅛ teaspoon hot pepper sauce

▶ Combine all ingredients in a jar; cover tightly and shake vigorously. Store in refrigerator. Shake before each use.
Yield: about ⅔ cup

Black-Eyed Pea Salad
5 ounces fusilli, bowtie, or shell pasta
2 cups frozen black-eyed peas, cooked and drained
⅔ cup chopped green bell pepper
½ cup thinly sliced green onions
¼ cup chopped fresh parsley
1 cup cherry tomatoes, halved
Green leaf lettuce
6 slices bacon, cooked and crumbled
Garnish: green onion fans

▶ Cook pasta according to package directions; drain. Rinse and drain again.
▶ Combine pasta, peas, bell pepper, green onions, parsley, and tomato halves in a large bowl; add Jalapeño Dressing to taste and toss to coat.
▶ Line a salad bowl or serving platter with lettuce. Spoon pasta mixture over lettuce and sprinkle with bacon. Serve at room temperature.
Yield: 6 servings

Rice and Artichoke Salad

To serve as an entree salad, add chicken or shrimp.

1 (6-ounce) package chicken-flavored rice
6 green onions, thinly sliced
½ green bell pepper, diced
12 pimiento-stuffed olives, sliced
2 (6-ounce) jars marinated artichoke hearts
¾ to 1 teaspoon curry powder
½ cup mayonnaise

▸ Cook rice according to package directions; set aside to cool.
▸ Combine green onions, bell pepper, and olives; add to cooled rice.
▸ Drain artichoke hearts, reserving marinade. Cut artichoke hearts into fourths. Combine reserved marinade, curry powder, and mayonnaise.
▸ Combine rice mixture and artichoke hearts in a large bowl. Add desired amount of mayonnaise mixture and toss to coat. Chill several hours before serving. Let stand at room temperature 1 hour before serving.

Yield: 6 to 8 servings

Caesar Pasta Salad

Sun-dried tomatoes lend a chewy texture and intense tomato flavor.

8 ounces corkscrew or rotini pasta
1 cup sun-dried tomatoes, cut in halves
1 large cucumber, seeded and chopped
½ cup chopped purple onion
1 red bell pepper, chopped
½ cup shredded Parmesan cheese
Pepper to taste
1 (8-ounce) bottle Caesar dressing

▸ Cook pasta according to package directions; drain. Rinse in cold water and drain again.
▸ Combine tomato halves and boiling water to cover in a small bowl; let stand 10 minutes or until softened. Drain well.
▸ Combine pasta, tomato halves, cucumber, onion, bell pepper, cheese, and pepper. Add desired amount of dressing, tossing to coat. Cover and chill 2 hours before serving.

Yield: 6 to 8 servings

Curry Rice and Bean Salad

For a tailgate picnic, serve this slightly sweet salad, Pork Tenderloin with Mustard Sauce (see page 109), rolls, crisp radishes, celery and carrot sticks.

Curry Dressing
⅔ cup mayonnaise
1 tablespoon curry powder
1 tablespoon honey
1 tablespoon apple cider vinegar
⅛ teaspoon ground red pepper
2 teaspoons prepared mustard
1 teaspoon Worcestershire sauce

▸ Whisk together all ingredients; cover and chill.
Yield: ¾ cup

Salad
1 (6-ounce) package long-grain and wild rice mix
Chicken broth
1 cup raisins
1 cup hot water
½ cup sliced green onions
1 cup chopped pecans, toasted
1 (16-ounce) can garbanzo beans, drained and rinsed
Lettuce leaves
Garnish: green onion fans
Curry Dressing

▸ Cook rice according to package directions, substituting chicken broth for specified amount of water.
▸ Combine raisins and 1 cup hot water; let stand 10 minutes. Drain.
▸ Add raisins, green onions, pecans, and beans to rice. Add desired amount of Curry Dressing and toss to coat.
▸ Arrange lettuce leaves on a serving platter and top with rice mixture; garnish, if desired. Serve warm or chilled.
Yield: 6 servings

Tabbouleh

This Middle Eastern salad, combining bulgur and the refreshing flavors of mint, parsley, and lemon, is delicious with grilled chicken and seafood. Bulgur, crushed wheat kernels, is available in health food stores and in the rice section at supermarkets.

2 cups boiling water
1 cup bulgur wheat
3 cups chopped tomato
1½ cups finely chopped fresh parsley
½ cup finely chopped fresh mint
½ cup chopped green onion or sweet onion
1 cup peeled, seeded, and chopped cucumber (optional)
⅓ to ½ cup fresh lemon juice
3 tablespoons extra-virgin olive oil
2 garlic cloves, crushed
1 teaspoon salt
½ teaspoon pepper
Pita bread or Processor Cracker Bread (see page 166)

▶ Pour 2 cups boiling water over wheat; let stand 1 hour. Drain in fine sieve.
▶ Combine wheat, tomato, parsley, mint, onion, and if desired, cucumber, in a large bowl.
▶ Combine lemon juice, oil, garlic, salt, and pepper in a small bowl; add to salad, tossing to coat.
▶ Cover salad and chill at least 1 hour before serving.
▶ Serve with pita or cracker bread.
Yield: 8 servings

Greek Coleslaw

A delicious intensely flavorful slaw.

1 (2-pound) cabbage, shredded (about 9 cups)
¾ cup vegetable oil
½ cup white vinegar
2 tablespoons Greek seasoning
1½ teaspoons pepper
1 (3-ounce) jar pimiento-stuffed olives, drained and sliced
1 (2½-ounce) can ripe olives, drained and sliced

▸ Place cabbage in a large bowl.
▸ Combine oil, vinegar, Greek seasoning, and pepper in a jar; cover tightly and shake vigorously. Add desired amount of dressing to cabbage and toss to coat.
▸ Serve immediately for crisper slaw or chill 8 hours or overnight for softer texture. Add olives just before serving.
Yield: 6 to 8 servings

Bleu Cheese Coleslaw

It's great with grilled meat or poultry.

3 tablespoons apple cider vinegar
2 tablespoons finely chopped onion
1 tablespoon sugar
¾ teaspoon celery seeds
¼ teaspoon salt
⅛ teaspoon dry mustard
¼ teaspoon pepper
1 garlic clove, minced
¼ cup vegetable oil
1 (1-pound) cabbage, finely shredded (about 4½ cups)
1 (4-ounce) package crumbled bleu cheese

▸ Combine first 9 ingredients in a jar; cover tightly and shake vigorously.
▸ Cover and refrigerate at least one hour.
▸ Combine cabbage and bleu cheese in a large bowl; cover and refrigerate 1 hour.
▸ Drizzle desired amount of vinegar mixture over cabbage mixture, tossing to coat. Serve immediately.
Yield: 4 to 6 servings

Crunchy Chinese Slaw with Soy Dressing

Napa cabbage, a variety of Chinese cabbage, has crinkly, thick-veined leaves that are cream-colored with light green tips. The leaves are thin and crisp with a mild, delicate flavor.

Soy Dressing
¼ cup apple cider vinegar
¾ cup vegetable oil
2 tablespoons soy sauce
½ cup sugar

▸ Bring all ingredients to a boil in a small saucepan over medium-high heat; cook, stirring constantly, until sugar dissolves. Remove from heat and let cool. Store in refrigerator. Shake before each use.

Yield: 1¼ cups

Slaw
½ cup butter
2 (3-ounce) packages chicken-flavored ramen noodles
1 (2.5-ounce) package slivered almonds
2 tablespoons sesame seeds
1 napa cabbage, finely shredded
1 bunch green onions, thinly sliced

▸ Melt butter in a large skillet over medium heat; add noodles, almonds, and sesame seeds and saute until lightly browned. Add seasoning packets and stir until coated. Remove from heat and let cool.

▸ Combine cabbage and green onions in a large bowl; chill. To serve, combine cabbage and noodle mixtures. Add desired amount of Soy Dressing and toss to coat.

Yield: 12 servings

Marsue's Creamy Coleslaw

Soaking the onions in ice water for several hours mellows their flavor.

Creamy Slaw Dressing
1½ cups mayonnaise
1½ teaspoons celery seeds
1 teaspoon dill seeds (optional)
1 tablespoon prepared mustard
3 tablespoons lemon juice
1½ tablespoons sugar

▸ Whisk together all ingredients. Chill.
Yield: about 2 cups

Slaw
1 medium onion, thinly sliced
1 (2-pound) cabbage, shredded (about 9 cups)
1 green bell pepper, thinly sliced (optional)
Salt and freshly ground pepper to taste

▸ Soak onion slices in ice water to cover several hours. Drain well.
▸ Combine cabbage, onion, and, if desired, bell pepper in a large bowl.
  Add desired amount of Creamy Slaw Dressing and toss to coat.
▸ Season slaw with salt and pepper to taste; serve chilled.
Yield: 6 to 8 servings

Cee's Caper Slaw

Capers, the flower buds of the Mediterranean caper bush, are sun-dried and pickled in a salty vinegar brine. Their pungent flavor adds piquancy to many dressings and sauces.

1 (3.5-ounce) jar capers
1 (2-pound) cabbage, thinly sliced (about 9 cups)
2 green onions, chopped
1 cup mayonnaise
Juice of 2 lemons
Freshly ground pepper to taste

▸ Drain capers, reserving juice.
▸ Combine cabbage, green onions, and 2 tablespoons capers in a large bowl; toss gently.
▸ Combine mayonnaise, lemon juice, pepper, and 2 tablespoons reserved caper juice in a small bowl.
▸ Add desired amount of dressing to cabbage mixture and toss well. Chill 8 hours or overnight, if desired. Serve immediately for crisp slaw.
Yield: 6 to 8 servings

Crunchy Broccoli Slaw

A clever way to get your family to eat broccoli

½ cup vegetable oil
⅓ seasoned rice vinegar
¼ cup sugar
1 teaspoon monosodium glutamate (optional)
1 teaspoon salt
1 teaspoon pepper
1 (16-ounce) package broccoli slaw
1 (10-ounce) package angel hair slaw
6 green onions, chopped
½ cup sunflower kernels
1 (2.25-ounce) package sliced almonds, toasted

▸ Combine first 6 ingredients in a jar; cover tightly and shake vigorously. Chill at least 6 hours.
▸ Combine broccoli slaw, angel hair slaw, green onions, sunflower kernels, and almonds in a large bowl; add desired amount of dressing and toss to coat.
Yield: 8 servings

Gazpacho Aspic

Don't let the number of ingredients scare you. It's so easy to make with a blender.

24 ounces tomato juice, divided
5 teaspoons unflavored gelatin (2 ½ envelopes)
1 large tomato, peeled and seeded
¼ white onion, quartered
1 medium cucumber, peeled and seeded
2 green onions, cut into 1-inch pieces
¼ teaspoon salt
¼ teaspoon ground white pepper
½ teaspoon hot sauce
½ teaspoon Worcestershire sauce
1 tablespoon lemon juice
3 tablespoons olive oil
1 tablespoon wine vinegar
½ teaspoon celery salt
Lettuce leaves
Sour cream

▸ Sprinkle gelatin over half of tomato juice in a 2-quart saucepan; let stand 2 minutes to soften. Bring to a simmer and stir until completely dissolved.
▸ Puree tomato, onion, cucumber, green onions, and remaining tomato juice in a blender until smooth; add to gelatin mixture. Stir in salt, pepper, hot sauce, Worcestershire sauce, lemon juice, oil, vinegar, and celery salt.
▸ Pour into a lightly oiled 6-cup mold and chill until firm.
▸ Unmold salad onto lettuce leaves and serve with sour cream.
Yield: 12 servings

Tomato-Lemon Ring

This tangy salad is good with chicken and seafood dishes.

1 envelope unflavored gelatin
1½ cups water, divided
1 (3-ounce) package lemon-flavored gelatin
1 (10½-ounce) can tomato soup
3 tablespoons lemon juice
1 teaspoon grated onion
⅓ cup sliced pimiento-stuffed olives
⅓ cup diced celery
Lettuce leaves

- Sprinkle unflavored gelatin over ¼ cup cold water; let stand 2 minutes to soften.
- Bring remaining 1¼ cups water to a boil in a medium saucepan; add lemon-flavored gelatin and softened unflavored gelatin, stirring until gelatin is dissolved.
- Whisk in tomato soup, lemon juice, and onion until smooth. Chill until consistency of unbeaten egg whites.
- Fold in olives and celery and pour into a lightly oiled 3½ to 4-cup ring mold. Chill until firm.
- Unmold salad onto a lettuce-lined serving platter.

Yield: 6 to 8 servings

Coronado Salad Ring

The horseradish gives this a subtle zing and refreshing flavor.

1 (3-ounce) package lime-flavored gelatin
1 (3-ounce) package lemon-flavored gelatin
2 cups boiling water
1¼ cups dry small curd cream-style cottage cheese
1 (20-ounce) can crushed pineapple, well drained
⅔ cup chopped walnuts or pecans
1 cup whipping cream
1 cup mayonnaise
1 tablespoon prepared horseradish
Fresh strawberries

- Combine first 3 ingredients in a large bowl, stirring until gelatin is dissolved.
- Add cottage cheese, pineapple, nuts, whipping cream, mayonnaise, and horseradish, stirring well.
- Pour into a 2-quart ring mold coated with vegetable cooking spray and chill until firm.
- Unmold salad onto a serving platter and fill center with fresh strawberries.

Yield: 8 to 10 servings

Gingered Peach Salad

Great for holiday menus, especially with ham and turkey.

1 (29-ounce) jar spiced peaches, undrained
1 (3-ounce) package orange-flavored gelatin
1 (3-ounce) package lemon-flavored gelatin
1 cup boiling water
1 cup cold water
1 tablespoon orange juice
1 tablespoon lemon juice
1¼ teaspoons ground ginger, divided
½ teaspoon salt
1 (8-ounce) can crushed pineapple, undrained
½ cup chopped apple
½ cup chopped pecans
½ cup sour cream
Lettuce leaves

▸ Drain peaches, reserving ¾ cup liquid. Pit and chop peaches and set aside.
▸ Combine orange- and lemon-flavored gelatins and 1 cup boiling water, stirring until gelatin is dissolved.
▸ Add reserved ¾ cup peach liquid, 1 cup cold water, orange juice, lemon juice, 1 teaspoon ginger, and salt to gelatin mixture, stirring well. Chill until consistency of unbeaten egg whites.
▸ Fold in chopped peaches, pineapple, apple, and pecans. Pour into a lightly oiled 9-inch square baking dish. Cover and chill.
▸ Combine sour cream and remaining ¼ teaspoon ginger, stirring well.
▸ Serve salad on lettuce-lined plates and top each serving with a dollop of sour cream mixture.
Yield: 8 servings

Apple Salad

It's a very good salad with or without the topping. The topping is also luscious on fresh fruit or pound cake.

Salad
1 (6-ounce) package lemon-flavored gelatin
2 cups boiling water
1 cup cold water
2 cups unpeeled, diced apple
1 (8.5-ounce) can crushed pineapple, undrained

2 cups miniature marshmallows
I cup chopped pecans

> Combine gelatin and 2 cups boiling water in a large bowl, stirring until gelatin is dissolved. Add I cup cold water, stirring well. Chill until the consistency of unbeaten egg white.
> Stir apple, pineapple, marshmallows, and pecans into gelatin mixture. Pour into a lightly oiled 13 x 9 x 2-inch baking dish. Cover and chill until firm.
> To serve salad, top with Creamy Fruit Topping or serve topping on the side.

Yield: 12 servings

Creamy Fruit Topping
2 large eggs, beaten
½ cup sugar
2 tablespoons lemon juice
I (1.3-ounce) envelope whipped topping mix

> Cook eggs, sugar, and lemon juice in a medium saucepan over low heat, stirring constantly, until thickened. Remove from heat and let cool.
> Prepare whipped topping mix according to package directions; fold into egg-sugar mixture.

Yield: about 2 cups

Frozen Cranberry Salad

Nice to have in the freezer for unexpected company

I (8-ounce) package cream cheese, softened
¼ cup sugar
I (16-ounce) can whole-berry cranberry sauce
I (15¼-ounce) can crushed pineapple, drained
I cup chopped pecans
I (8-ounce) container frozen whipped topping

> Beat cream cheese and sugar at medium speed with an electric mixer until creamy.
> Fold in cranberry sauce, pineapple, pecans, and whipped topping.
> Place foil-lined baking cups in muffin pan.
> Spoon salad into cups. Cover and freeze until firm. Transfer frozen salads in foil-lined cups to a covered container or heavy-duty zip-top plastic bag to store until ready to serve.
> Let salads stand at room temperature 15 minutes before serving.

Yield: 12 servings

Green Green Fruit Salad

Add strawberries for holiday color and serve this refreshing, low-fat salad in a fancy crystal bowl.

Citrus-Mint Fruit Dressing
½ fresh orange juice
¼ cup fresh lemon juice
¼ cup tightly packed fresh mint leaves, chopped
3 tablespoons sugar (optional)

▸ Combine all ingredients in a small bowl; cover and chill 1 hour.
Yield: about 1 cup

Fruit Salad
2 medium kiwi, peeled and thinly sliced
1 cup seedless green grapes
1 small pear, cut into ½-inch pieces
1 cup honeydew melon balls
Garnish: fresh mint sprigs

▸ Combine first 4 ingredients in a large glass bowl; add desired amount of Citrus-Mint Fruit Dressing and toss gently. Garnish, if desired.
Yield: 4 servings

Winter Fruits with Balsamic Citrus Dressing

Balsamic vinegar, made from white grapes, has a pungent sweetness. A splash of balsamic enhances the flavor of out-of-season fruits.

Balsamic Citrus Dressing
¼ cup vegetable oil
¼ cup fresh orange juice
3 tablespoons balsamic vinegar
1 tablespoon honey
⅛ teaspoon cracked pepper

▸ Combine all ingredients in a jar; cover tightly and shake vigorously. Chill until ready to serve.

Yield: about ¾ cup

Fruit Salad
2 pears, cut into wedges
2 teaspoons lemon juice
1 head leaf lettuce
2 pink grapefruit, peeled and sectioned
2 oranges, peeled and cut crosswise into 8 slices
1 cup red or green seedless grapes

▸ Brush pear wedges with lemon juice.
▸ Place lettuce on a large serving platter; arrange pear, grapefruit, orange, and grapes on top. Cover with plastic wrap and chill up to 4 hours.
▸ Drizzle with desired amount of Balsamic Citrus Dressing when ready to serve.

Yield: 8 servings

Buttermilk-Bleu Cheese Dressing

This cool and creamy salad dressing helps tame the heat of a spicy hot entree.

½ cup mayonnaise
¼ cup sour cream
1½ tablespoons cider vinegar
1½ tablespoons fresh lemon juice
¼ teaspoon hot sauce
½ teaspoon minced garlic
1 teaspoon salt
½ teaspoon freshly ground pepper
¾ cup buttermilk
1 (3 to 4-ounce) package crumbled bleu cheese or Roquefort cheese

▸ Combine first 8 ingredients in a bowl; whisk in buttermilk. Stir in cheese. Cover and chill several hours.
▸ Serve dressing over mixed greens.
Yield: 2 cups

NOTE: ¾ cup (3 ounces) finely shredded cheddar cheese and a dash of Worcestershire sauce may be substituted for bleu cheese.

Wimberly Hory House Dressing

Try this oriental-style dressing on mixed greens with fruit.

1 cup vegetable oil
1 cup plus 1½ tablespoons cider vinegar
1 cup sugar
1 tablespoon Accent
1 tablespoon Mei Yen Seasoning (we prefer Spice Island)
1¼ teaspoons salt
¾ tablespoon pepper
1 clove garlic, crushed or whole

▸ Combine all ingredients in a jar, cover tightly, and shake vigorously. Store in refrigerator. Shake before each use.
Yield: 2¼ cups

NOTE: You can substitute 1 tablespoon of Beau Monde seasoning plus 1½ teaspoons of salt for Mei Yen seasoning.

Soups & Sandwiches

Playtime

Imagination Place Children's Museum

It's another busy morning in Imagination Place.
Children dress in feather boas and top hats for a tea party.
A brother and sister build a computer-modeled skyscraper.
A future doctor studies Operating Annie's heart and lungs.
In the Science Hall, classmates reach out to feel the swirling
winds of a miniature tornado.

At first glance, Imagination Place Children's Museum appears to be
just an elaborate playground. But a closer look reveals that the
museum helps children learn about their world through role-playing
and hands-on discovery.

Located in the historic Kyle Building adjacent to the Center for Cultural
Arts, Imagination Place is divided into KidsTown USA and the Science
Hall. KidsTown includes a child-sized health clinic, fire station,
grocery store, bank, construction site and Grandma's two-story house
- all built along a miniature main street. Inside each shop, games and
activities teach life-lessons such as choosing nutritious food and being
responsible with money.

The Science Hall includes exhibits like a desert-making machine, a
ten-foot tornado and a light spectrum. In this area, young visitors can
experiment with mirrors, shadows, lightning, wind and the colors of
the rainbow.

Learning opportunities don't end here. Full-time teachers and
volunteer docents present educational programs to more than 35,000
students each year. One of the most popular is Star Lab, a portable
planetarium where students climb inside to learn basic astronomy and
sky lore, while marveling at stars and celestial images.

Imagination Place reinforces the widely held notion that the best
lessons come from play that encourages children to think, dream and
discover. Whether playing on their own or participating in group
activities, a visit to the Children's Museum always adds spark to the
imagination.

Cream of Lettuce Soup

This colorful soup is perfect for a ladies luncheon.

2 pounds romaine lettuce, coarsely chopped
1 teaspoon salt
¼ cup fresh or frozen green peas
6 tablespoons butter
½ cup minced green onions
¼ cup all-purpose flour
Salt and freshly ground pepper
1 quart chicken stock (Easy Chicken Stock, see page 96)
¼ teaspoon dried chervil
¼ teaspoon dried thyme
½ to 1 teaspoon salt
1 cup whipping cream
Garnish: shredded lettuce

▸ Cook lettuce in boiling salted water to cover in a Dutch oven 6 to 7 minutes; add peas and cook 3 to 4 more minutes or until lettuce is wilted. Drain.

▸ Melt butter in a Dutch oven over medium heat; add green onions and sauté until tender. Add flour, stirring well, and cook 1 to 2 minutes.

▸ Add lettuce, peas, and salt and pepper to taste; cook, stirring constantly, 2 to 3 minutes.

▸ Gradually stir in chicken stock.

▸ Process soup in a blender in batches, 2 to 3 cups at a time, until desired consistency.

▸ Return soup to Dutch oven and add chervil, thyme, and ½ to 1 teaspoon salt. Cook over medium heat until thoroughly heated. Add whipping cream to taste.

▸ Serve soup hot or cold. Garnish, if desired.

Yield: 3 quarts

Gazpacho

A cool soup for a hot summer day

2 large tomatoes, peeled and divided
1 large cucumber, peeled and divided
1 medium onion, divided
1 medium-size green bell pepper, seeded and divided
1 (46-ounce) can tomato juice, divided
¼ cup olive oil
⅓ cup red wine vinegar
¼ teaspoon hot sauce
1 teaspoon salt
¼ teaspoon garlic powder
¼ teaspoon coarsely ground pepper
Croutons

▸ Coarsely chop half of each of the first 4 ingredients. Process vegetables and 1 cup tomato juice in a blender until smooth.
▸ Combine the pureed vegetables with the remaining tomato juice, oil, vinegar, hot sauce, salt, garlic powder, and pepper. Mix well, cover, and chill for at least 2 hours.
▸ Dice the remaining tomato, cucumber, onion, and bell pepper. Place in small serving bowls to serve as accompaniments.
▸ Serve soup in chilled bowls and top with diced vegetables and croutons, if desired.

Yield: about 10 cups

White Bean and Fresh Tomato Soup

Pesto is sauce of fresh herbs, garlic, Parmesan cheese, and olive oil.

Soup
1½ cups dried navy beans
13 cups water
12 fresh sage leaves or 1½ teaspoons dried sage, divided
6 garlic cloves, chopped and divided
6 bay leaves, divided
8 thyme branches or ½ teaspoon dried thyme, divided
2 teaspoons salt, divided
4 tablespoons olive oil, divided
3 cups finely chopped yellow onion
2 pounds ripe tomatoes, peeled, seeded, and chopped
Salt and pepper to taste

- Sort and wash beans; place in a large Dutch oven and add water to 2 inches above beans. Let soak 8 hours. Drain well and return to Dutch oven.
- Add 13 cups water and half each of sage, garlic, bay leaves, thyme, salt and 1 tablespoon oil. Bring to a boil; cover, reduce heat, and simmer 1 hour or until beans are tender but not mushy.
- Remove from heat and pour mixture through a wire-mesh strainer, reserving broth. Set aside.
- Cook onion and remaining sage, garlic, bay leaves, thyme, salt, and 3 tablespoons hot oil in a Dutch oven over medium heat for 8 to 10 minutes or until onion is translucent.
- Add tomato and 10 cups reserved broth; bring to a boil. Cover, reduce heat, and simmer 20 minutes.
- Add beans and simmer 10 minutes or until thoroughly heated. Remove and discard bay leaves, sage leaves, and thyme branches.
- Season with salt and pepper to taste. Garnish with Parsley Pesto.

Yield: 9 cups

Parsley Pesto

1 cup fresh parsley leaves, finely chopped and divided
2 garlic cloves
¼ teaspoon salt
3 tablespoons extra-virgin olive oil
3 tablespoons freshly grated Parmesan cheese
Red wine vinegar to taste

- Process garlic in a food processor until minced; add 2 tablespoons chopped parsley, salt, and oil and process until a smooth paste forms.
- Transfer mixture to a bowl; stir in cheese, remaining minced parsley, and vinegar to taste.

Yield: about ¾ cup

Creamy Broccoli Soup

Potatoes rather than a rich cream sauce thicken this soup.

2 tablespoons butter
1 cup chopped onion
2 cups broccoli florets and sliced peeled stalk
2 medium potatoes, peeled and diced
5 cups chicken broth
1 tablespoon chopped fresh parsley
Grated rind and juice of 1 lemon
Salt and pepper to taste
¾ cup crème fraîche, sour cream, or yogurt

▸ Melt butter in a Dutch oven over medium heat; add onion and sauté until tender.

▸ Add broccoli, potatoes, broth, and parsley and bring to a boil. Cover, reduce heat, and simmer 15 to 20 minutes or until vegetables are tender. Remove from heat and let cool to room temperature.

▸ Process vegetable mixture with broth, in batches, 2 to 3 cups at a time, in a food processor or blender until smooth. Return to Dutch oven; add lemon juice and salt and pepper to taste.

▸ Cook soup over medium heat, stirring often, until thoroughly heated. Serve with crème fraîche and sprinkle with lemon rind.

Yield: 8 cups

French Onion Soup

The secret is slowly cooking the onions until they are sweet and golden brown.

3 tablespoons butter
1 tablespoon olive oil
1 pound onions, sliced into thin rings
Pinch of sugar
½ teaspoon salt
2 tablespoons all-purpose flour
3 cups chicken broth
3 cups beef broth
⅓ cup dry red wine
Freshly ground pepper to taste
6 (¾-inch thick) French bread slices
4 ounces Gruyère cheese, thinly sliced
4 ounces fresh Parmesan cheese, thinly sliced

- Melt butter in a Dutch oven over medium heat; add oil and heat. Add separated onion rings, stirring well. Cover and cook 15 minutes.
- Add sugar and salt to onion and cook 30 more minutes or until onion is deep golden brown, stirring occasionally.
- Sprinkle flour over onion and cook, stirring constantly, 2 to 3 minutes. Gradually add broths and wine, stirring constantly.
- Bring soup to a boil; reduce heat and simmer 30 minutes. Season with pepper to taste.
- Broil bread 3 inches from heat (according to oven manufacturer's directions) on both sides until lightly browned. Top each slice evenly with cheese. Broil until cheese is melted and bubbly.
- Ladle soup into serving bowls and top each bowl with a slice of bread. Serve immediately.

Yield: 6 servings

Corn Chowder

"It's our ultimate comfort food."

1 medium onion, thinly sliced
4 cups diced, peeled potato (½-inch cubes)
1 cup water
4 cups fresh corn kernels or 1 (20-ounce) cylinder frozen yellow creamed corn, thawed
1 cup whipping cream
1 tablespoon sugar
¼ cup butter
2 cups whole milk
2 teaspoons salt
Freshly ground pepper to taste

- Bring first 3 ingredients to a boil in a Dutch oven. Cover, reduce heat, and simmer 10 minutes or until potatoes are tender. Remove from heat.
- Combine corn, cream, sugar, and butter in a 2-quart saucepan; cook over medium heat about 10 minutes or until corn is tender.
- Add corn mixture, milk, salt, and pepper to potato mixture; cook over low heat, stirring occasionally, until thoroughly heated. Do not boil.

Yield: 3 quarts

VARIATION: For Chicken-Corn Chowder, add 1 cup chopped cooked chicken and ½ cup crumbled cooked bacon to soup. Cook until thoroughly heated.

Quick and Easy Brunswick Stew

For this tasty stew, pick up an order of "inside, outside chopped" meat from your favorite barbeque joint.

6 cups peeled, diced potatoes
2 tablespoons butter
1 large onion, chopped
1 (20-ounce) cylinder frozen yellow creamed corn, thawed
1 (28-ounce) can diced tomatoes
1 (10-ounce) can premium white chicken
⅓ pound shredded pork barbeque (about 1¼ cup)
⅓ pound shredded beef barbeque (about 1¼ cup)
2 tablespoons ketchup or to taste
2 tablespoons barbeque sauce or to taste
2 tablespoons Worcestershire sauce
¼ cup soy sauce
1 to 2 tablespoons fresh lemon juice or to taste
1 teaspoon black pepper
1 to 2 teaspoons hot sauce
1 (14½-ounce) can chicken broth (optional)

▸ Cook potatoes in boiling water to cover in a Dutch oven 10 minutes or until tender; drain.
▸ Melt butter in Dutch oven over medium heat; add onion and sauté until tender. Add corn and cook over low heat 5 minutes or until corn is tender.
▸ Add potatoes, tomatoes, chicken, meat, ketchup, barbeque sauce, Worcestershire sauce, soy sauce, lemon juice, pepper, and hot sauce to Dutch oven; bring to a boil over medium heat. Reduce heat and simmer, stirring occasionally, 30 minutes.
▸ Add chicken broth to thin, if desired.
Yield: 4 quarts

Tortilla-Chicken Soup

Serve this brothy soup with Stuffed Broiled Avocados (see page 136) and a tossed green salad.

1 small onion, chopped
2 celery stalks, diced
2 tablespoons vegetable oil
4 bone-in chicken breasts, cooked and shredded
4 (14.5-ounce) cans chicken broth
1 (10-ounce) can diced tomatoes and green chiles

¼ to ½ cup chopped fresh cilantro
½ teaspoon garlic salt
Tortilla chips
2 cups (8 ounces) shredded Monterey Jack cheese
Fresh lime slices (optional)

▸ Sauté onion and celery in hot oil in a Dutch oven over medium heat until onion is translucent.
▸ Add chicken, broth, and diced tomatoes, stirring well. Add cilantro and garlic salt; reduce heat and simmer 30 minutes.
▸ Crumble a handful of tortilla chips in each bowl; top with ¼ cup cheese. Ladle soup over chips and cheese. Squeeze each serving with lime juice, if desired.

Yield: about 4 quarts

Santa Fe Soup

Super easy! After cooking the beef and onion, add the remaining ingredients and simmer for 2 hours.

2 pounds lean ground chuck
1 large onion, chopped
2 (1-ounce) envelopes Ranch dressing mix
2 (1.25-ounce) envelopes taco seasoning mix
2 (11-ounce) cans yellow shoepeg corn, drained
2 cups water
1 (15-ounce) can black beans, undrained
1 (15-ounce) can pinto beans, undrained
1 (15-ounce) can kidney beans, undrained
1 (14.5-ounce) can diced tomatoes, undrained
1 (10-ounce) can diced tomatoes and green chiles, undrained
Toppings: cheese, sour cream

▸ Cook ground chuck and onion in a large Dutch oven over medium heat, stirring until it crumbles and is no longer pink; drain.
▸ Add Ranch dressing mix, taco seasoning mix, corn, 2 cups water, beans, and tomatoes to Dutch oven and bring to a boil. Cover, reduce heat, and simmer, stirring occasionally, 2 hours.
▸ Garnish each serving with desired toppings. Serve with tortilla chips or cornbread. Best if made ahead.

Yield: about 3 quarts

Chad's Chili

For an extremely hot and distinctive flavor, add habanero chile sauce.

3 pounds ground round
¼ cup butter or margarine
2 medium onions, chopped
2 garlic cloves, minced
2 jalapeño peppers, seeded and chopped
1 celery stalk, diced
2 (12-ounce) cans beer
1 (28-ounce) can diced tomatoes
2 (8-ounce) cans tomato sauce
1 (10-ounce) can diced tomatoes and green chiles
1 (32-ounce) can chili hot beans
1 (8-ounce) can water chestnuts, drained and diced
1 (10¾-ounce) can beef broth
2 (16-ounce) packages prepared chili con carne
2 teaspoons chili powder
1 teaspoon ground red pepper
Salt to taste
Habanero chili sauce (optional)

- ▸ Cook beef in a large Dutch oven over medium heat, stirring until it crumbles and is no longer pink. Drain and set aside.
- ▸ Melt butter in Dutch oven over medium heat; add onions, garlic, pepper, and celery and sauté, stirring often, until tender.
- ▸ Return beef to Dutch oven, add beer, diced tomatoes, tomato sauce, diced tomatoes and green chiles, chili hot beans, water chestnuts, beef broth, chili con carne, chili powder, ground red pepper, salt, and, if desired, habanero chili sauce. Reduce heat and simmer, stirring occasionally, 2 hours.

Yield: 4 quarts
NOTE: *The packages of chili con carne, often referred to as chili logs, are available in the meat or frozen food department.*

White Chicken Chili

A package of gravy mix lends rich flavor and creamy texture.

½ pound dried navy beans
3 tablespoons butter
1 large onion, chopped
3 garlic cloves, minced (optional)
2 to 3 teaspoons chili powder
1 teaspoon dried oregano
1 teaspoon ground cumin
1 teaspoon ground white pepper
1 (14½-ounce) can chicken broth, divided
1 (1.2-ounce) envelope roasted chicken gravy mix
2 cups half-and-half
1 teaspoon hot sauce
2 (4.5-ounce) cans chopped green chiles, drained
3 cups chopped cooked chicken
Toppings: sour cream, salsa, shredded Monterey Jack cheese

▸ Sort and wash beans; place in a large Dutch oven and add water to 2 inches above beans. Let soak 8 hours. Drain well and return to Dutch oven.

▸ Add water to cover and bring to a boil; cover, reduce heat, and simmer 1 hour or until beans are tender but not mushy. Drain and set aside.

▸ Melt butter in Dutch oven over medium heat; add onion and, if desired, garlic and sauté until tender. Add chili powder, oregano, cumin, and pepper and cook 1 minute.

▸ Combine 1 cup chicken broth and gravy mix in a jar; cover tightly and shake vigorously; gradually add to onion mixture with remaining broth and cook over medium-high heat, stirring constantly, until thoroughly heated.

▸ Gradually add half-and-half, stirring constantly, and cook until thoroughly heated. Reduce heat and simmer 5 minutes or until thickened.

▸ Add hot sauce, green chiles, chicken, and beans; cover and simmer 30 minutes. If desired, add additional chicken broth for thinner consistency.

▸ Serve with desired toppings.

Yield: 4 quarts
NOTE: Substitute chicken broth for part of the half-and-half, if desired.

Ray's Easy Chili

Even a novice will have great success with this chili.

3 pounds ground round
3 medium onions, chopped
3 tablespoons vegetable oil
3 (10-ounce) cans whole tomatoes and green chiles, undrained
3 (14½-ounce) cans Mexican-style stewed tomatoes, undrained
3 (32-ounce) cans chili hot beans, drained
3 (1.75-ounce) envelopes chili seasoning mix

▸ Cook beef in a Dutch oven over medium heat, stirring until it crumbles and is no longer pink. Drain and set aside.
▸ Sauté onion in hot oil in Dutch oven over medium heat until translucent.
▸ Add beef, tomatoes, beans, and seasoning mix to onion. Bring to a boil; cover, reduce heat to low, and simmer, stirring occasionally, 2 hours.
Yield: 6 quarts

Texas Chili con Carne

This Texas-style chili garnered a blue ribbon in a chili cookoff. Chorizo, a Mexican sausage, is made with coarsely chopped fresh pork and seasoned with garlic and chili powder.

8 ounces chorizo sausage, casings removed
2 pounds sirloin tips, trimmed and cut into bite-size pieces
1½ cups chopped onion
2 garlic cloves, minced
2 to 3 jalapeño peppers, seeded and chopped
1½ to 2 tablespoons chili powder
½ to 1 teaspoon crushed red pepper
½ teaspoon salt or to taste
¼ teaspoon dried oregano
2 bay leaves
2 cups water
1 (12-ounce) can tomato paste
1 (16-ounce) can tomatoes, chopped
2 (15.5-ounce) cans pinto beans, drained
Toppings: shredded longhorn cheese, sour cream, salsa, chopped onion

▸ Cook chorizo in a large Dutch oven over medium heat, stirring until it crumbles and is no longer pink. Drain, reserving drippings in Dutch oven.

Set sausage aside.

▸ Cook sirloin tips, onion, garlic, and jalapeño in hot reserved drippings in Dutch oven over medium heat until tips are browned.

▸ Add sausage, chili powder, red pepper, salt, oregano, bay leaves, 2 cups water, tomato paste, tomatoes, and beans and bring to a boil. Cover loosely, reduce heat to low, and simmer 3 hours, stirring occasionally.

▸ Remove and discard bay leaves. Serve with desired toppings.

Yield: 3 quarts

Jan's Chili

A very thick chili with a rich combination of flavors.

2 pounds ground chuck
2 medium onions, chopped (about 1 cup)
1 small green bell pepper, chopped
1 (15-ounce) can red kidney beans, drained
1 (15-ounce) can chili hot beans, undrained
1 (15-ounce) can New Orleans-style beans, undrained
1 (8-ounce) can baked beans
2 (14.5-ounce) cans diced tomatoes, drain reserving liquid
1 (6-ounce) can tomato paste
1 (8-ounce) cans tomato sauce
3 (1.75-ounce) envelopes chili seasoning mix (2 with onion bits and 1 hot)

▸ Cook beef in a large Dutch oven over medium heat, stirring until it crumbles and is no longer pink. Drain, reserving drippings in Dutch oven, and set aside.

▸ Sauté onion and bell pepper in hot reserved drippings in Dutch oven over medium heat until tender.

▸ Add beef, beans, tomatoes, tomato paste, tomato sauce, and chili seasoning mix to Dutch oven, stirring well; reduce heat to low and simmer, stirring occasionally, 2 hours. Add reserved tomato liquid or water, if necessary, to prevent sticking.

Yield: 1 gallon

Easy Chicken Stock

Soups are best made with richly-flavored stocks. Enhance the flavor of canned chicken broth with this easy idea.

3 (14-ounce) cans chicken broth
2 carrots, thinly sliced
1 small onion, thinly sliced
¼ cup white wine
4 sprigs fresh parsley
4 fresh thyme sprigs or 1 teaspoon dried thyme

▸ Combine all ingredients in a large saucepan. Bring to a boil, reduce heat, and simmer for 30 minutes. Strain. Substitute for homemade stock.
Yield: about 5 cups

Mediterranean Chicken Sandwich

Perfect for your left-over chicken

1½ cups diced cooked chicken (about 6 ounces)
½ cup diced ripe or pimiento-stuffed olives
½ cup chopped red bell pepper
⅓ cup chopped green onions
¼ cup regular or reduced-calorie mayonnaise
1 tablespoon red wine vinegar
1 garlic clove, minced
½ teaspoon dried oregano, crumbled
Salt and pepper to taste
½ (16-ounce) French bread loaf

▸ Combine first 4 ingredients in a medium bowl.
▸ Whisk together mayonnaise, vinegar, garlic, and oregano in a small bowl; add to chicken mixture, tossing to coat. Season with salt and pepper to taste.
▸ Cut bread in half lengthwise and remove soft center, leaving a ½-inch shell on top and bottom. Spoon salad into bottom half, spreading evenly.
▸ Cover with top half and press to compact slightly. Cut into 2-inch sections and serve.
Yield: 2 servings

Muffuletta Sandwich

Olive salad is the unique ingredient of this New Orleans specialty.

Olive Salad
2 garlic cloves
1 (10-ounce) jar pimiento-stuffed olives, drained
1 (7¾-ounce) jar or can ripe olives, drained
1 small onion
¼ cup fresh parsley
1 carrot (optional)
1 red bell pepper (optional)
4 celery stalks (optional)
2 teaspoons dried oregano or dried Italian seasoning
¼ teaspoon dried red pepper flakes
2 to 4 tablespoons olive oil
2 tablespoons white wine vinegar

▸ Process garlic in a food processor until finely chopped. Add olives, onion, parsley, and, if desired, carrot, bell pepper, and celery and process until coarsely chopped.
▸ Add oregano and remaining ingredients, stirring well. Cover and chill 8 hours or up to 1 week.
Yield: 4 to 5 cups

Sandwich
Prepared mustard (optional)
1 (10-inch) round Italian bread loaf, cut in half horizontally
¼ to ½ pound thinly sliced ham
4 to 6 ounces sliced provolone cheese
1 to 1½ cups Olive Salad
¼ pound sliced hard Genoa salami

▸ Spread mustard on bread, if desired. Layer ham and cheese on bottom half of bread. Top with Olive Salad and salami. Top with remaining bread half.
▸ Serve at room temperature or wrap in aluminum foil and bake at 350° for 15 to 20 minutes or until thoroughly heated.
Yield: 3 to 4 servings
NOTE: 1 (12-ounce) jar mixed pickled garden vegetables, drained, may be substituted for carrot, bell pepper, and celery in Olive Salad, if desired.

Cajun Chicken Sandwich

Good and spicy!

¼ cup teriyaki sauce
¼ cup red wine
1½ teaspoons dried thyme
1 teaspoon ground red pepper
1 teaspoon ground black pepper
1 teaspoon ground white pepper
1 teaspoon garlic powder
4 skinned and boned chicken breast halves (about 1 pound)
1 tablespoon olive oil
¼ cup mayonnaise
1 tablespoon prepared horseradish
8 (1-inch) French bread slices, toasted
2 cups coarsely shredded lettuce

▸ Combine first 7 ingredients in a shallow baking dish.
▸ Place chicken between 2 sheets of plastic wrap and pound to ¼-inch thickness or cut chicken into strips.
▸ Place chicken in marinade, turning to coat. Cover and chill 2 to 4 hours. Remove chicken from marinade, discarding marinade.
▸ Cook chicken in hot oil in a large skillet over medium-high heat 2½ to 4 minutes on each side or until chicken is done.
▸ Combine mayonnaise and horseradish in a small bowl; spread 1 side of each bread slice with mixture and top with lettuce. Place chicken on lettuce and top with remaining bread slice.

Yield: 4 servings
NOTE: *To grill chicken breasts, grill over medium-high heat 4 minutes on each side or until chicken is done. Proceed as directed above.*

Brick Press Sandwich

Great tailgate fare for the Etowah Youth Orchestra's Spring Concert at Mort Glosser Amphitheatre

1½ teaspoons Dijon mustard
¼ cup extra-virgin olive oil
1 tablespoon balsamic vinegar
Salt and pepper to taste
1 (16-ounce) rustic Italian bread loaf (we prefer ciabatta)
1 (4.5-ounce) jar prepared black olive paste, divided
4 ounces peppered hard salami, thinly sliced
3 medium-size roasted red bell peppers, cut into 1-inch slices
4 to 6 ounces goat cheese or 8 ounces feta or shredded mozzarella cheese
1 (8-ounce) jar marinated artichoke hearts, drained and chopped
6 ounces prosciutto, thinly sliced, or smoked country ham,
   sliced and parboiled
2 ¼ cups loosely packed mixed fresh herbs (basil, parsley, or arugula)

▸ Whisk together first 3 ingredients; season with salt and pepper to taste and refrigerate.

▸ Cut bread in half lengthwise and remove soft center, leaving a ½-inch shell on top and bottom halves. Reserve center bread for another use.

▸ Spread bottom half of bread with half of olive paste; top with salami and bell pepper slices. Crumble cheese over bell pepper slices and top with artichoke hearts. Place prosciutto over artichoke hearts.

▸ Spread remaining olive paste over the inside of the top bread half and place over prosciutto.

▸ Wrap sandwich in plastic wrap and place a brick on top. Chill 2 hours or overnight.

▸ Remove from refrigerator and let stand at room temperature 2 hours before serving. Just before serving, remove top and arrange fresh herbs over meat and drizzle with Dijon vinaigrette. Cut into 1-inch-thick slices.

Yield: 10 servings

Cheese Rectangles

These party cheese sandwiches are a perfect accompaniment to soups and salads.

2 (5-ounce) jars Old English cheese spread, softened
¾ cup butter, softened
1 large egg, lightly beaten
20 white or whole wheat bread slices, with crusts trimmed
Paprika

▸ Beat first 3 ingredients at medium speed with an electric mixer until creamy; spread mixture on 10 bread slices. Top with remaining bread slices and cut each sandwich in half, forming 20 rectangles.

▸ Spread 5 sides of each rectangle with cheese mixture, leaving bottom plain. Place on a greased baking sheet and sprinkle with paprika.

▸ Bake at 375° for 10 to 15 minutes or until lightly browned.

Yield: 20 sandwiches

Hot Ham and Cheese Sandwiches

Wrap in aluminum foil and chill; your family can bake sandwiches as needed.

½ cup mayonnaise
2½ teaspoons dried Italian seasoning
½ teaspoon freshly ground pepper
6 hoagie rolls
1 cup thinly sliced onion
1 medium-size green bell pepper, cut into thin strips
1 celery stalk, sliced
1 tablespoon olive oil
⅔ to 1 pound thinly sliced deli ham
1 cup (4 ounces) shredded mozzarella cheese
1 cup (4 ounces) shredded cheddar cheese

▸ Combine first 3 ingredients in a small bowl; spread insides of each roll with 2 teaspoons mixture.
▸ Sauté onion, bell pepper, and celery in hot oil in a large skillet over medium-high heat just until tender.
▸ Arrange ham evenly on bottom halves of rolls; top each evenly with sautéed vegetables.
▸ Combine mozzarella and cheddar cheeses and sprinkle ⅓ cup on each sandwich. Place top half of roll over cheeses. Wrap sandwiches individually in aluminum foil.
▸ Bake at 375° for 15 to 20 minutes or until thoroughly heated.
Yield: 6 sandwiches
NOTE: 1 (16-ounce) round sourdough bread loaf may be substituted for hoagie rolls. Slice off top one-third and hollow out bottom portion leaving a ½-inch shell, reserving center portion for another use. Proceed as directed above. Bake sandwich at 375° for 30 minutes or until thoroughly heated.

Grilled Eggplant and Tomato Sandwich

Delectable combo of charcoal-grilled summer vegetables, herbs, and melted cheese

3 Japanese or small young eggplants (about 12 ounces)
Salt and pepper to taste
⅓ cup olive oil
2 garlic cloves, minced
¼ cup chopped fresh basil
4 (½-inch thick) Italian bread slices, cut diagonally
1 large tomato, cut into ¼-inch slices
4 (1-ounce) fontina, Swiss, or mozzarella cheese slices
Fresh basil leaves

▸ Cut Japanese eggplant in half lengthwise or cut regular eggplant into ½-inch slices. Sprinkle slices generously with salt and let stand 5 minutes. Pat dry.

▸ Combine oil, garlic, and chopped basil in a small bowl. Season with salt and pepper to taste.

▸ Brush eggplant, bread, and tomato slices with oil mixture.

▸ Grill eggplant over medium-high heat 14 minutes, turning frequently, or until tender and slightly charred. Place bread and tomato slices on grill during last 3 minutes and cook until bread is golden and tomato slices begin to soften, turning once.

▸ Transfer 2 bread slices to a plate. Top remaining bread slices on the grill evenly with eggplant, cheese, tomato, and basil leaves. Cover and grill 1 minute or just until cheese melts. Transfer sandwiches to plates and top with bread slices. Serve immediately.

Yield: 2 sandwiches

Centerstage

CenterStage Presents . . .

For budding musicians, playwrights, singers and actors, finding an audience is a challenge. Thanks to CenterStage Presents, the performing arts division of the Center for Cultural Arts, talented artists and enthusiastic audiences have found each other.

Since its beginning in 1991, CenterStage Presents has evolved from sponsoring occasional dinner theatres and musical performances to include a summer-long concert series.

Because of this program, the Gadsden community has been entertained by an eclectic array of cultural events including many locally-produced plays such as A. R. Gurney's *Love Letters* and touring productions like the *Great American River Tour*, which celebrates the days of Mark Twain.

As spring arrives, CenterStage enters its busiest time of the year. Every weekend all summer long, the Center's New Orleans-style courtyard fills with people. They gather in this downtown hideaway for a chance to relax with friends in the evening air. Thanks to the Serendipity Dance Club, the walls of the courtyard come to life with trompe l'oeil paintings. As the popularity of the series grows, so do the number of audition tapes by blues, jazz, classical, bluegrass and rock musicians.

So whether art-lovers are on stage in an original play or listening to bluegrass from a table for two, they help the CenterStage Presents program achieve its goal - to bring together artist and audience.

Flank Steak with Horseradish Cream

A simple herb-and-spice mixture rubbed on the marinated steak creates a flavorful meal, and great sandwiches if you have any leftovers.

Flank Steak

¼ cup bourbon
2 tablespoons soy sauce
1 (1½-pound) flank steak, trimmed
1 teaspoon salt
2 teaspoons onion powder
2 tablespoons chili powder
2 tablespoons paprika
2 teaspoons pepper
2 teaspoons garlic powder
1 tablespoon olive oil

▸ Combine bourbon and soy sauce in a heavy-duty zip-top plastic bag; add steak and seal. Chill 24 hours, turning bag occasionally.
▸ Combine salt, onion powder, chili powder, paprika, pepper, and garlic powder in a small bowl.
▸ Drain steak, discarding marinade. Pat steak dry and rub with oil. Rub with chili powder mixture. Cover and chill 30 minutes.
▸ Coat food rack with vegetable cooking spray. Place steak on grill over medium-high heat (350° to 400°); grill 6 to 8 minutes on each side or until desired degree of doneness. Do not overcook.
▸ Cut steak diagonally across grain into thin slices. Serve with Horseradish Cream.
Yield: 4 to 6 servings

Horseradish Cream

½ cup plain yogurt or sour cream
3 tablespoons prepared horseradish
1 teaspoon Dijon mustard
1 garlic clove, minced

▸ Combine all ingredients in a bowl, stirring well. Cover and chill.
Yield: ⅔ cup

Steak "n" Wine Gravy

Great for a crowd on a cold winter night.

¼ cup butter
1½ pounds fresh mushrooms, sliced
2 to 3 pounds sirloin tip, cut into 1-inch cubes
1 tablespoon vegetable oil
1 cup beef broth or consommé, divided
¾ cup red wine
2 tablespoons soy sauce
½ medium onion, grated
2 garlic cloves, minced
2 tablespoons all-purpose flour
½ (10¾-ounce) can cream of mushroom soup, undiluted
Salt to taste
Hot cooked rice or noodles

▸ Melt butter in a skillet over medium-high heat; add mushrooms and sauté about 5 minutes or until tender. Transfer mushrooms and pan juices to a large bowl.

▸ Brown sirloin cubes in hot oil in skillet over medium heat. Add sirloin to mushrooms, reserving drippings in skillet.

▸ Add ¾ cup broth, wine, soy sauce, onion, and garlic to drippings in skillet. Bring to a boil.

▸ Combine flour and remaining ¼ cup beef broth, stirring until smooth. Gradually stir into wine mixture. Cook, stirring constantly, until mixture is smooth and thickened. Add mushroom soup, stirring until smooth. Add salt to taste.

▸ Add mushrooms and sirloin cubes to sauce. Reduce heat, cover, and simmer, stirring occasionally, 1 hour to 1 hour and 15 minutes or until tender.

▸ Serve over hot cooked rice or noodles.
Yield: 6 to 8 servings

Mesquite Grilled Beef Tenderloin

You'll have your guests standing in line for this!

1 (4 to 6 pound) beef tenderloin, trimmed
1½ cups Merlot
3 tablespoons olive oil
1 teaspoon salt
¾ teaspoon freshly ground pepper
Mesquite wood chips

▸ Combine tenderloin and Merlot in a heavy-duty zip-top plastic bag. Seal and chill 24 hours, turning bag occasionally.
▸ Remove tenderloin from marinade, discarding marinade. Rub with oil and sprinkle with salt and pepper.
▸ Prepare wood chips according to package directions and sprinkle over hot coals to cool them down.
▸ Brown tenderloin over high heat, turning often.
▸ Grill tenderloin over low heat (under 300°), turning occasionally, 30 to 45 minutes or until a meat thermometer inserted into thickest portion registers desired degree of doneness.

Yield: 8 to 10 servings

Roasted Beef Tenderloin

"This is our family's traditional Christmas specialty."

½ cup butter
6 green onions, chopped
3 beef bouillon cubes
2 tablespoons red wine vinegar
1 (5 to 6 pound) beef tenderloin, trimmed

▸ Melt butter in a skillet over medium heat; add green onions and sauté until tender. Add bouillon, stirring until dissolved. Remove from heat and stir in red wine vinegar.
▸ Place tenderloin on a rack in shallow pan, tucking thin end under. Pour green onion mixture over top. Let stand 15 minutes.
▸ Bake at 425° for 30 to 35 minutes, basting with green onion mixture frequently until a meat thermometer inserted into thickest portion registers desired degree of doneness.
▸ Let stand at room temperature 10 minutes before serving.

Yield 10 to 12 servings

Meat Balls in Cabbage Leaves

"It's a traditional favorite when my family comes home."

2 large cabbages
3 ½ pounds lean ground chuck
1 medium onion, chopped and divided
3 large eggs, lightly beaten
½ cup matzo meal or fine, dry breadcrumbs
2 teaspoons salt
1 teaspoon pepper
6 celery stalks, chopped
3 (28-ounce) cans whole tomatoes, coarsely chopped
1 (8-ounce) can tomato sauce
1 (6-ounce) can tomato paste
2 cups firmly packed light brown sugar
½ teaspoon white vinegar

- Core cabbages. Steam each until tender.
- Drain and cool about 15 to 20 minutes.
- Combine chuck, half of onion, eggs, meal, salt, and pepper. Roll into small (¼ cup) logs. Place each log at the bottom of a large cabbage leaf, turn sides over and roll (egg roll-style).
- Coarsely chop the remaining cabbage; add celery and remaining onion.
- Place half of cabbage mix in large roasting pan. Layer cabbage rolls and cover with remaining chopped cabbage mixture.
- Combine tomatoes, tomato sauce, tomato paste, light brown sugar, and vinegar in a large bowl. Blend and pour over cabbage.
- Cover, bake at 300° for 3 hours.

Yield: 18 servings

NOTE: This freezes very well.

Beef Stroganoff

Freeze the meat for about an hour - just until slightly firm - for easier slicing.

¼ cup butter, divided
2 medium onions, thinly sliced
1 (8-ounce) package fresh mushrooms, sliced
1 pound beef round or sirloin, cut into ¼-inch wide strips
2 tablespoons all-purpose flour
1 garlic clove, minced
3 to 4 medium tomatoes, peeled and chopped with juice reserved
1½ teaspoons salt
¼ teaspoon Worcestershire sauce
⅛ teaspoon pepper
Dried oregano to taste
½ cup sour cream
Hot cooked rice or noodles

▸ Melt 2 tablespoons butter in a heavy skillet over medium heat; add onion and sauté until browned. Add fresh mushrooms and cook 5 minutes. Transfer onion and mushrooms to a bowl.

▸ Melt remaining 2 tablespoons butter in skillet over medium heat; add beef and cook until browned. Add garlic and flour, coating meat. Cook and stir 2 minutes. Add chopped tomato and juice, salt, Worcestershire sauce, pepper, and oregano. Cover, reduce heat, and simmer 1 hour, stirring occasionally.

▸ Return onion and mushrooms to skillet; simmer 30 minutes. Stir in sour cream just before serving. Do not boil.

▸ Serve over hot cooked rice or noodles.

Yield: 4 to 6 servings

NOTE: 1 (4-ounce) can sliced mushrooms, drained, may be substituted for fresh mushrooms. Proceed as directed above.

Baked Chimichangas

Traditionally, a chimichanga is a fried burrito. For a healthy and easy supper, these are baked.

½ pound lean ground beef or 3 boneless chicken breast halves cut in
   ½-inch pieces
2 tablespoons chopped green bell pepper
½ cup quick cook rice
2 tablespoons sliced ripe olives
¾ cup salsa
1 teaspoon chili powder
1 (5.6-ounce) package refrigerated taco salad shells, at room temperature
1 cup (4 ounces) shredded cheddar cheese
Toppings: Guacamole (see page 135), salsa, sour cream, shredded lettuce,
   diced tomato

▸ Cook ground beef or chicken pieces and bell pepper in a large skillet over medium heat, stirring until no longer pink. Drain.

▸ Return meat or chicken and bell pepper to skillet. Add rice, olives, salsa, and chili powder; bring to a boil. Reduce heat and simmer 5 minutes.

▸ Spoon one-fourth of the meat mixture in the middle of each salad shell; top with ¼ cup cheese. Fold in 2 sides of shell to enclose filling. Fold over top and bottom edges, forming rectangles. Secure with wooden picks.

▸ Place chimichangas, folded side down, on a lightly greased baking sheet.

▸ Bake at 375° for 16 to 20 minutes or until browned. Remove wooden picks.

▸ Serve chimichangas with desired toppings.

Yield: 4 servings

NOTE: 4 (8-inch) flour tortillas may be substituted for taco salad shells. Spray chimichangas with cooking spray and bake at 425° for 8 minutes. Turn chimichangas and bake 5 more minutes or until lightly browned.

Pork Tenderloin with Mustard Sauce

Best served on small yeast rolls - it's been a hit at our Annual Auction.

Pork Tenderloin
½ cup teriyaki marinade and sauce (we prefer Kikkoman)
¼ cup bourbon
2 tablespoons brown sugar
2 garlic cloves, minced
2 (1½-pound) pork tenderloins, trimmed

▸ Combine first 4 ingredients, stirring well. Combine marinade mixture and tenderloins in a 13 x 9 x 2-inch baking dish. Cover and chill 6 to 8 hours, turning occasionally.
▸ Bake at 400° for 20 to 25 minutes or until a meat thermometer inserted into thickest portion registers 160°, basting frequently with pan drippings.
▸ Let stand at room temperature 15 minutes before serving. Thinly slice tenderloin and serve on rolls with Mustard Sauce.
Yield: 10 servings

Mustard Sauce
3 tablespoons dry mustard
1 tablespoon teriyaki marinade and sauce (we prefer Kikkoman)
1 tablespoon white vinegar
1 cup sour cream
¾ cup mayonnaise
2 tablespoons chopped green onions

▸ Whisk together first 3 ingredients, adding a drop or two more of teriyaki marinade or vinegar if mixture is too dry. Whisk in sour cream and mayonnaise. Fold in green onions.
Yield: about 2 cups

NOTE: *Tenderloins may also be grilled. Remove from marinade, reserving marinade. Bring reserved marinade to a boil, simmer 4 minutes. Grill tenderloins over medium heat (300° to 350°) 15 to 20 minutes or until a meat thermometer inserted into thickest portion registers 160°, basting frequently with reserved marinade and turning occasionally.*

Lamb à la Grecque

The delectable, lemony, herb and olive oil marinade is suitable for any cut of lamb, chicken or pork.

Greek-Style Marinade
Grated rind of 1 lemon
½ cup fresh lemon juice
3 garlic cloves, minced
2 tablespoons dried oregano, crushed
¼ cup finely chopped fresh parsley
1 tablespoon coarse-grain sea salt
1 teaspoon coarsely ground pepper
¾ cup olive oil

▸ Combine first 7 ingredients in a bowl, stirring well with a fork. Add oil, stirring with a fork until well blended.

Marinated Lamb
1 (5 to 6-pound) leg of lamb

▸ Score fat side of lamb or make 8 to 10 slits with the point of a paring knife.
▸ Combine lamb and Greek-Style Marinade in a heavy-duty zip-top plastic bag. Seal and chill 8 hours or overnight, turning bag occasionally.
▸ Remove from refrigerator and let stand at room temperature 2 hours before cooking.
▸ Place lamb and marinade in a shallow roasting pan.
▸ Bake at 350° for 1 hour and 30 minutes basting frequently with pan drippings or until a meat thermometer inserted into thickest portion registers desired degree of doneness.
▸ Remove from oven and tent with foil. Let stand at room temperature 15 minutes before carving.
Yield: 6 to 8 servings

Ham-a-Glisten

A sweet and sour pineapple sauce enhances the ham.

1 (2 to 2½-pound) center-cut ham slice
1 tablespoon butter
1 tablespoon apple cider vinegar
¼ cup honey
1 tablespoon Worcestershire sauce
¼ teaspoon ground ginger
1 (8-ounce) can crushed pineapple

▸ Place ham in a shallow baking dish.
▸ Melt butter in a heavy saucepan over low heat; add vinegar, honey, Worcestershire sauce, ginger, and crushed pineapple. Simmer, stirring constantly, 3 minutes. Pour over ham slice.
▸ Bake at 350° for 1 hour and 30 minutes, basting occasionally with pan drippings.
Yield: 6 servings

Southwestern Chicken

It's good and easy! Serve with rice or in a taco shell with shredded lettuce.

6 skinned and boned chicken breast halves
1½ cups Italian dressing
1 teaspoon minced garlic
¾ teaspoon pepper
4 to 6 green onions, thinly sliced
2 to 3 tomatoes, diced
¾ cup (3 ounces) shredded mozzarella cheese
¾ cup (3 ounces) shredded cheddar cheese

▸ Pierce chicken with a fork; place in a shallow dish or a heavy-duty zip-top plastic bag. Add dressing, garlic, and pepper; cover or seal and chill 1 hour, turning once.
▸ Remove chicken from marinade, discarding marinade. Place chicken in a 13 x 9 x 2-inch greased baking dish.
▸ Bake at 350° for 20 to 25 minutes or until tender. Remove from oven and top evenly with green onions, tomatoes, and cheeses. Bake 4 to 5 more minutes or until cheese is melted.
Yield: 6 servings
NOTE: *Marinated chicken can be grilled rather than baked.*

Chicken Sauté with Mushroom Sauce

Easy, flavorful sauce

4 skinned and boned chicken breast halves
Salt and pepper to taste
All-purpose flour
2 to 4 tablespoons olive oil
2 (8-ounce) packages fresh mushrooms, sliced
4 garlic cloves, chopped
1 teaspoon dried oregano
1½ cups chicken broth
¼ cup lemon juice
¼ cup white wine
Chopped fresh parsley

▸ Wash chicken and pat dry. Place chicken between 2 sheets of wax paper or in a heavy-duty zip-top plastic bag. Flatten to ½-inch thickness using a meat mallet or the bottom of a small skillet. Season with salt and pepper. Dust chicken breasts with flour.
▸ Sauté chicken in hot oil in a large skillet over medium-high heat 4 minutes on each side or until evenly browned, shaking pan often to move chicken around.
▸ Transfer chicken to a platter, reserving drippings in skillet; season chicken with salt and pepper, if desired.
▸ Add mushrooms, garlic, and oregano to pan drippings. Cook 5 to 10 minutes or until tender.
▸ Add broth, lemon juice, and wine to mushroom mixture. Cook, stirring to loosen browned particles. Bring to boil. Reduce heat and simmer 5 minutes or until slightly thickened.
▸ Return chicken to skillet and simmer 5 minutes or until thoroughly heated.
▸ Transfer chicken and sauce to a serving platter and sprinkle with parsley.
▸ Serve with hot cooked rice or noodles.
Yield: 4 servings

The Best Southern Fried Chicken

"My children will drive from Atlanta if I mention frying a batch of this chicken."

Fried Chicken
3 quarts water
½ cup kosher salt or coarse-grain sea salt
1 (2 to 2½-pound) whole chicken, cut up
2 cups buttermilk
1 teaspoon salt
1 teaspoon pepper
1 cup all-purpose flour
2 tablespoons cornstarch
½ pound lard
¼ cup unsalted butter
2 bacon slices

▸ Combine 3 quarts water and kosher salt in a large bowl; add chicken. Cover and chill 4 to 8 hours. Drain chicken and rinse bowl.
▸ Return chicken to bowl and add buttermilk. Cover and chill 4 to 8 hours. Drain chicken on a wire rack; discard buttermilk.
▸ Combine 1 teaspoon salt and pepper; sprinkle half of mixture over all sides of chicken.
▸ Combine remaining salt and pepper mixture, flour, and cornstarch in a heavy-duty zip-top plastic bag; place 2 pieces of chicken in bag and seal. Shake to coat. Repeat procedure with remaining chicken pieces.
▸ Heat lard, butter, and bacon in a 12-inch cast-iron skillet or chicken fryer to 360° (a small cube of bread should brown in 60 seconds). Remove and discard bacon.
▸ Place chicken skin side down in grease, a few pieces at a time. Cover and cook 6 minutes. Uncover and cook 9 more minutes. Turn chicken; cover and cook 6 minutes. Uncover and cook 5 to 9 minutes, turning pieces during last 3 minutes for even browning, if necessary.
▸ Drain chicken on a paper towel-lined plate placed over a large bowl of hot water. Serve with Fried Chicken Gravy.
Yield: 4 servings

Fried Chicken Gravy
¼ cup all-purpose flour
¼ cup reserved pan drippings from The Best Southern Fried Chicken
2 cups milk or water, heated
½ teaspoon salt
¼ teaspoon pepper

▸ Stir flour into hot pan drippings in a skillet over medium heat. Cook, stirring constantly, until browned.
▸ Gradually add warm milk; cook, stirring constantly, 3 to 5 minutes or until thickened and bubbly. Stir in salt and pepper and serve immediately.
Yield: 1⅔ cups

Oven-Roasted Chicken

The perfect comfort food

½ **lemon**
1 **(4-pound) whole chicken**
Salt and pepper to taste
1 **small onion**
3 **fresh thyme sprigs**
1 **bay leaf**
1 **fresh rosemary sprig**
1 **fresh parsley sprig**
2 to 4 **tablespoons butter, softened**
1 **cup water or chicken broth**

▸ Rub lemon inside the chicken cavity. Sprinkle cavity with salt and pepper. Insert onion and herbs.

▸ Tie ends of legs together with string; tuck wingtips under. Place chicken in a roasting pan, breast side up. Rub skin with butter.

▸ Bake at 350° for 1 hour or until a meat thermometer inserted into thigh registers 180°, basting frequently with pan drippings.

▸ Transfer chicken to a serving platter, reserving drippings in pan. Tent aluminum foil over chicken.

▸ To make sauce, strain drippings using a gravy strainer; discard fat. Place roasting pan over medium-high heat; whisk in 1 cup water, stirring to loosen browned particles. Bring to a boil. Reduce heat and simmer until liquid is reduced to about half or until slightly thickened.

▸ Serve roasted chicken with sauce.

Yield: 4 servings

Greek Chicken with Orzo

Orzo is a tiny, rice-shaped pasta.

¼ cup fresh lemon juice
3 tablespoons water
1 teaspoon olive oil
1 teaspoon dried oregano
¼ teaspoon freshly ground pepper
2 garlic cloves, crushed
2 teaspoons Greek seasoning, divided
4 skinned and boned chicken breast halves
1 cup uncooked orzo
¼ cup ripe olives, sliced
1½ teaspoons chopped fresh chives
1 tablespoon butter or margarine, melted
½ teaspoon salt
Garnish: fresh oregano sprigs

▸ Combine first 6 ingredients and 1 teaspoon Greek seasoning in a heavy-duty zip-top plastic bag; add chicken and shake to coat. Chill 30 minutes, turning bag occasionally.

▸ Cook orzo according to package directions, omitting salt and oil. Drain. Add olives, chives, butter, salt, and remaining 1 teaspoon Greek seasoning, tossing well. Keep warm.

▸ Place chicken on grill over medium-high heat. Cook covered for 7 to 8 minutes on each side or until done, basting occasionally with marinade.

▸ Serve chicken over orzo. Garnish if desired.

Yield: 4 servings

Velvety Chicken Casserole

It's easy - gravy mix lends the velvety texture and tasty flavor.

2 (9-ounce) packages frozen artichoke hearts
¼ cup butter, divided
1 (8-ounce) package fresh mushrooms, sliced
3½ cups chopped cooked chicken
2 envelopes chicken gravy mix (we prefer French's)
1¼ cups (5 ounces) shredded Swiss cheese
¼ teaspoon dried marjoram
3 tablespoons dry sherry
1 cup soft breadcrumbs

- Cook artichokes according to package directions; drain and cut in half.
- Melt 2 tablespoons butter in a skillet over medium-high heat; add mushrooms and sauté 5 minutes.
- Combine artichokes, mushrooms, and chicken in a greased 13 x 9 x 2-inch baking dish.
- Prepare gravy according to package directions. Add cheese and marjoram, stirring until blended. Remove from heat and stir in sherry. Pour over chicken mixture.
- Melt remaining 2 tablespoons butter in skillet over medium heat; remove from heat. Add breadcrumbs, tossing to coat. Sprinkle over casserole.
- Bake at 350° for 40 minutes or until thoroughly heated.

Yield: 8 servings

Creamy Chicken Enchiladas with Salsa

The Fresh Tomato Salsa is delicious - but if you must, substitute commercial salsa.

3 cups shredded cooked chicken
2 cups (8 ounces) shredded cheddar cheese
1 (16-ounce) container sour cream
1 teaspoon salt (optional)
1 (4.5-ounce) can chopped green chiles, drained
12 (8-inch) flour tortillas
Toppings: shredded cheddar cheese, Fresh Tomato Salsa

▸ Combine first 5 ingredients, stirring well.
▸ Spoon ¼ heaping cup chicken mixture down the center of each tortilla. Roll up and place, seam side down, in a greased 13 x 9 x 2-inch baking dish.
▸ Bake at 350° for 20 to 30 minutes or until thoroughly heated.
▸ To serve: Sprinkle additional cheddar cheese over top or spoon Fresh Tomato Salsa over top.
Yield: 6 servings

Fresh Tomato Salsa
3 (4-ounce) cans chopped green chiles, drained
1 garlic clove, minced
2 tablespoons olive or vegetable oil
1½ pounds ripe tomatoes, peeled and chopped
2 cups chopped onion
1 teaspoon salt
½ teaspoon dried oregano
½ cup water
½ cup fresh cilantro, chopped (optional)

▸ Sauté chiles and garlic in hot oil in a skillet over medium heat. Add tomatoes, onion, salt, oregano, and ½ cup water. Reduce heat and simmer 30 minutes. Stir in cilantro, if desired.
Yield: 5 to 6 cups

White Barbeque Sauce Chicken

This versatile sauce is delicious served with grilled pork or smoked chicken.

White Barbeque Sauce
2 cups mayonnaise (we prefer Kraft)
⅓ cup apple cider vinegar
¼ cup fresh lemon juice
2 tablespoons sugar
1 tablespoon coarsely ground pepper
2 tablespoons white wine Worcestershire sauce

▸ Combine all ingredients in a small bowl. Use as marinade and sauce for chicken.

Yield: 3 cups

Grilled Chicken
6 skinned and boned chicken breast halves
White Barbeque Sauce

▸ Place chicken in a heavy-duty zip-top plastic bag or a shallow dish; add ½ cup White Barbeque Sauce, tossing to coat. Seal or cover and chill 30 minutes.
▸ Remove chicken from marinade, discarding marinade.
▸ Coat food rack with vegetable cooking spray; place on grill over medium heat (300° to 350°). Place chicken on rack and grill 7 to 8 minutes on each side or until done.
▸ Serve chicken with remaining sauce.

Yield: 6 servings

Roscoe's Barbeque Chicken

This is the old-fashioned way of slow cooking with frequent basting.

1 (10-ounce) jar mustard sauce (we prefer Durkee's)
6 lemons, sliced
1 cup vinegar
1 cup butter or margarine
2 tablespoons dry mustard
2 tablespoons sugar
2 tablespoons salt
10 chicken halves

▸ Cook first 7 ingredients in a saucepan over medium heat, stirring until butter is melted.
▸ Grill chicken over medium-high heat for 10 minutes on each side. Lower heat to low and cook for 1½ to 2 hours, basting with sauce every 15 minutes, until juices run clear.

Yield: 10 servings

Wayne's Smoked Lemon Chicken

Leftovers make great sandwiches with White Barbeque Sauce (see page 118), lettuce, and tomato.

4 (3 to 3½-pound) whole chickens (try to have all about the same size)
4 lemons
Seasoned salt
Black pepper
Lemon pepper

▸ Wash chickens and pat dry. Place 1 lemon in the cavity of each chicken. Rub the skin with salt and peppers.
▸ Prepare smoker according to manufacturer's directions.
▸ Place 2 chickens on upper rack and 2 chickens on lower rack. Cover with smoker lid.
▸ Cook 4 to 5 hours (at least 1 hour per pound of chicken) or until juices run clear and a thermometer inserted into thickest part of breast registers 180°.
▸ Remove lemon before serving.

Yield: 8 to 12 servings

Smoked Cornish Hens

Rubbing the herb mixture under the skin and in the cavity allows the flavors to permeate the flesh.

4 Cornish hens
1 tablespoon salt
1 tablespoon dried rosemary, crushed
2 teaspoons pepper
4 garlic cloves
2 lemons, halved
4 to 6 ounces hickory chips

- Rinse hens in cold water and allow to drain.
- Combine salt, rosemary, and pepper.
- Rub each hen cavity with a garlic clove. Using 2 teaspoons herb mixture for each bird, sprinkle in the cavity, under, and on the skin. Squeeze half of a lemon into each cavity and leave lemon half in cavity.
- Prepare smoker according to manufacturer's directions.
- Add hickory chips.
- Place hens, breast side up, on rack. Cover with smoker lid.
- Cook 45 minutes. Turn hens and cook 60 more minutes or until a meat thermometer inserted into thickest part of breast registers 185°.
- Let cool a few minutes. Split hens in half lengthwise, discarding lemon halves.

Yield: 8 servings

Colonel Curl's Quail Wraps

Soaking game in buttermilk "tames" the wild flavors and tenderizes the meat.

8 quail, dressed
1 cup buttermilk (or to cover)
1 cup soy-based marinade (We prefer Dale's)
8 apple-smoked bacon slices, halved
16 pickled jalapeño slices
16 water chestnut slices
Hickory chips

▶ Remove breasts from quail and cut each breast in half.
▶ Place breast halves in a bowl and add buttermilk to cover. Chill 8 hours. Drain quail and rinse bowl.
▶ Return quail to bowl and add soy-based sauce. Chill 8 hours. Drain.
▶ Place 1 jalapeño slice and 1 water chestnut slice on each breast piece; fold over and wrap with half a bacon slice. Secure with a wooden pick.
▶ Soak hickory chips in water to cover 30 minutes (soak chunks 1 hour).
▶ Prepare charcoal fire in smoker on one side of grill, leaving other side empty; let burn 15 to 20 minutes.
▶ Place quail on food rack over hot coals and sear 5 minutes, turning frequently. (Watch for flare-ups because of bacon.) Move quail to empty side of grill.
▶ Drain chips and place on coals. Cover with lid, opening vent over quail to pull hickory flavor over.
▶ Cook 15 minutes or until done.
Yield: 4 servings

Jambalaya Stir-Fry

Wow! True Cajun flavor from a wok!

2 tablespoons lite soy sauce
2 tablespoons fresh lemon juice
2 teaspoons cornstarch
3 tablespoons vegetable oil
1 garlic clove, minced
1 cup green onions, thinly sliced
1 large green bell pepper, cut into ⅛-inch strips
1 large red bell pepper, cut into ⅛-inch strips
¾ cup chopped cooked ham
1 pound medium-size fresh shrimp, peeled and deveined
6 to 8 ounces cooked crawfish tail meat (optional)
1 tablespoon chili powder
¼ teaspoon dried crushed red pepper (optional)
Hot steamed rice
¼ cup sliced or slivered almonds, toasted

▸ Combine first 3 ingredients in a small bowl, stirring until smooth. Set aside.
▸ Heat oil in a heavy skillet or wok over medium-high heat. Add garlic, green onions, and bell peppers. Stir-fry 3 minutes or until vegetables are crisp-tender.
▸ Stir in ham. Add shrimp and stir-fry, stirring constantly, 2 minutes or until shrimp turn pink.
▸ Add chili powder and, if desired, crushed red pepper and stir-fry 1 minute. Add soy sauce mixture and cook until mixture is slightly thickened.
▸ Serve over hot steamed rice and sprinkle with toasted almonds.
Yield: 4 to 6 servings

Shrimp Baked with Feta

Easy and delicious shrimp entrée

½ cup chopped onion
3 tablespoons olive oil
4 garlic cloves, minced
1 (28-ounce) can diced tomatoes, drained
¼ cup clam juice
¼ cup Chablis or other white wine
1 tablespoon Pernod or other licorice-flavored liqueur (optional)
¼ teaspoon salt
¼ teaspoon freshly ground black pepper
1 teaspoon dried whole oregano
1 teaspoon dried crushed red pepper
1 pound large fresh shrimp, peeled and deveined, or scallops
4 ounces feta cheese, crumbled
½ cup pitted ripe olives (optional)
2 tablespoons chopped fresh parsley
Hot cooked pasta or rice

- Sauté onion in hot oil in a large skillet over medium-high heat until tender; add garlic and cook 1 minute. Add chopped tomatoes, clam juice, wine, and, if desired, Pernod. Cook over high heat 1 minute or until boiling. Cover, reduce heat, and simmer 15 minutes. Stir in salt, black pepper, oregano, and red pepper; set aside.
- Pour tomato mixture into a greased shallow 2-quart baking dish. Arrange shrimp over sauce. Sprinkle with feta and, if desired, olives.
- Bake at 425° for 15 minutes or until cheese is melted and shrimp turn pink. Do not overcook. Remove from oven and sprinkle with parsley.
- Serve over hot cooked pasta or rice.

Yield: 4 servings

NOTE: This dish can be assembled in advance, covered, and refrigerated 8 hours or overnight. Let stand at room temperature 1 hour before baking. For individual servings, layer ingredients in individual baking dishes and bake 10 minutes or until shrimp turn pink.

Shrimp Curry

For a foolproof, perfectly smooth sauce, heat the milk before adding it to the butter and flour mixture.

6 tablespoons butter
½ cup minced onion
1 tablespoon curry powder
⅓ cup all-purpose flour
1 (14½-ounce) can chicken broth
2 cups milk, heated
1½ teaspoons salt
¼ teaspoon ground ginger
1 teaspoon lemon juice
¼ to ½ teaspoon crushed red pepper (optional)
3 pounds medium-size fresh shrimp, peeled and deveined
Hot cooked rice
Condiments: raisins, salted almonds or peanuts, sautéed onion slices, pineapple tidbits, chopped hard-cooked egg, cooked and crumbled bacon, flaked coconut, chutney

▸ Melt butter in a Dutch oven over medium heat; add onion and sauté 5 minutes or until crisp-tender. Add curry powder and flour, stirring until smooth. Cook, stirring constantly, 1 minute.
▸ Gradually add chicken broth and milk; cook, stirring constantly, over medium heat until thickened and bubbly. Stir in salt, ginger, lemon juice, and, if desired, red pepper. Add shrimp and cook 3 to 4 minutes or until shrimp turn pink. Do not overcook.
▸ Serve over hot cooked rice with desired condiments.
Yield: 6 servings
NOTE: 4 cups chopped cooked chicken may be substituted for shrimp.

Shrimp Noel

Don't wait for Christmas to try this easy, elegant dish.

¼ cup butter or margarine
2 (8-ounce) packages fresh mushrooms, sliced
I cup chopped onion
I cup chopped green bell pepper
3 cups cooked rice
I (6-ounce) can crabmeat
I (4-ounce) jar chopped pimento
I teaspoon salt
I teaspoon chili powder
¼ to ½ cup butter or margarine, melted
1½ pounds medium fresh shrimp, cooked, peeled and deveined

▸ Melt ¼ cup butter in a large skillet over medium heat; add mushrooms, onion, and bell pepper and sauté until tender.
▸ Add rice and remaining ingredients to skillet, stirring well. Pour into a 2-quart baking dish.
▸ Bake at 300° for 50 minutes or until thoroughly heated.
Yield: 4 servings

Balsamic Basil Marinade

Superb one-hour marinade for grouper

⅓ cup olive oil
¼ cup tomato sauce
2 tablespoons balsamic vinegar
2 garlic cloves, crushed
2 tablespoons chopped fresh basil
½ teaspoon salt
½ teaspoon ground red pepper

▸ Combine all ingredients in a bowl, stirring well.
Yield: approximately ¾ cup

Red Snapper Veracruz

When snapper is not available, try this with cod or halibut.

2 medium onions, sliced
2 garlic cloves, minced
¼ cup olive oil
3 medium tomatoes or 6 plum tomatoes, coarsely chopped
2 small lemons, sliced
1 cup chopped fresh parsley
2 pounds red snapper fillets
Salt and pepper to taste
2 (4-ounce) cans whole green chiles, cut into strips, or 4 fresh jalapeño or poblano chile peppers, finely chopped
Garnishes: whole jalapeño peppers, fresh parsley sprigs, pimento-stuffed olives

▶ Sauté onion and garlic in hot oil in a large saucepan over medium-high heat 10 minutes or until lightly-browned, stirring constantly. Add tomatoes, lemon slices, and parsley. Simmer 5 minutes. Taste and adjust seasonings as desired.
▶ Sprinkle fish fillets with salt and pepper. Arrange in an single layer in a lightly oiled 13 x 9 x 2-inch baking dish; pour sauce evenly over top. Arrange peppers on top.
▶ Bake at 400° for 15 minutes or until opaque. Transfer to a warmed serving platter and garnish, if desired.
Yield: 4 servings

Lemon Marinade

Marinating for a week brings out the oils from the rinds to lend a rich lemon flavor.

3 lemons, each cut into 8 wedges
⅓ cup kosher salt
Juice of 1 lemon
Olive oil

▶ Pack lemon wedges in a quart-size jar. Add salt and juice of 1 lemon. Pour oil to 1 inch above lemon wedges. Store in refrigerator 1 week, turning daily.

Roasted Salmon with Salsa Verde

Sealing the fish in heavy-duty aluminum foil "steams" it to lock in the flavorful juices. It's an easy and clean method to prepare fish.

Roasted Salmon
1 (2 to 3-pound) salmon fillet
Salt and pepper to taste
1 large lemon, cut into thin slices
6 sprigs fresh oregano, basil, rosemary, and/or thyme
3 tablespoons olive oil
Garnishes: fresh herbs, lemon slices, lettuce

▸ Cut 2 (18 x 36-inch) pieces of heavy-duty aluminum foil. Place 1 piece on a 15 x 10-inch jelly-roll pan. Coat foil with vegetable cooking spray.
▸ Place salmon diagonally on foil; season with salt and pepper to taste. Top with lemon slices and fresh herbs; drizzle with oil.
▸ Coat remaining piece of foil with cooking spray; place, greased side down, over salmon and fold to seal.
▸ Bake salmon at 350° for 45 minutes or until a meat thermometer inserted into thickest portion registers 150° or fish flakes easily with a fork.
▸ Remove top sheet of foil; spoon juices into a small saucepan and bring to a boil. Boil 4 minutes or until reduced to about ½ cup. Remove from heat and cool. Cover and chill 8 hours or overnight. Reserve salmon juice for Salsa Verde.
▸ Cover salmon and chill 8 hours or overnight.
▸ To serve, remove salmon skin and scrape off dark meat. Arrange on a serving platter and garnish, if desired. Serve with Salsa Verde.
Yield: 6 servings

Salsa Verde
1¾ cups extra virgin olive oil
¼ cup fresh lemon juice
1½ cups chopped fresh parsley
½ cup chopped green onions
1 (3-ounce) jar capers, drained
1½ tablespoons chopped garlic
1½ teaspoons chopped fresh thyme
1½ teaspoons chopped fresh oregano
¾ teaspoon chopped fresh rosemary
¾ teaspoon chopped fresh sage
½ cup reduced salmon juice

▸ Whisk together first 10 ingredients; stir in reduced salmon juice. Chill.
Yield: about 3 cups

Thai Marinade

Use as a basting sauce or marinade for beef, chicken or pork.

5 large shallots, chopped
⅓ cup soy sauce
1½ tablespoons white vinegar
3 tablespoons minced fresh gingerroot
1½ tablespoons peanut oil
3 garlic cloves, minced
1½ teaspoons dark brown sugar
¾ teaspoon ground red pepper
1½ teaspoons ground coriander (optional)

▸ Combine all ingredients in a bowl, stirring well. Cover and chill.
Yield: about 1⅔ cups

Pasta Sauce Raphael

Artichoke hearts make this sauce distinctive.

2 (6-ounce) jars marinated artichoke hearts
2 cups chopped yellow onion
¼ cup olive oil
2 tablespoons minced garlic
½ teaspoon dried oregano
½ teaspoon dried basil
1 tablespoon coarsely ground black pepper
½ teaspoon salt
Pinch of dried red pepper flakes
1 (28-ounce) can diced tomatoes
¼ cup freshly grated Parmesan cheese
¼ cup chopped fresh parsley
1 pound angel hair pasta, cooked

▸ Drain artichokes, reserving liquid. Cut into quarters.
▸ Sauté onion in hot oil in a Dutch oven over medium-high heat 5 minutes or
  until translucent. Add garlic, oregano, basil, black pepper, salt, and red
  pepper; sauté 2 minutes.
▸ Add tomatoes to onion mixture; cover and simmer 30 minutes. Add
  artichoke quarters, Parmesan cheese, and parsley, stirring well. Simmer
  5 more minutes or until thoroughly heated.
▸ Combine tomato sauce and hot cooked pasta in a large bowl, tossing well
  to coat.
Yield: 5 to 6 servings

Rigatoni with Tomatoes, Olives, and Two Cheeses

Preparing the sauce ahead saves time and makes this an easy last-minute dish.

Tomato Sauce
1½ cups chopped onion
3 tablespoons olive oil
1 teaspoon minced garlic
3 (28-ounce) cans whole tomatoes, drained
2 (14½-ounce) cans low-sodium chicken broth
2 teaspoons dried basil
1 teaspoon dried crushed red pepper

▸ Sauté onion in hot oil in a Dutch oven over medium-high heat until translucent. Add garlic and cook 1 minute.
▸ Add tomatoes, broth, basil, and red pepper to skillet, stirring well. Bring to a boil; reduce heat to low and simmer 1 hour and 10 minutes, breaking up tomatoes with the back of a spoon as you stir occasionally. Reduce to about 6 cups.
▸ Season with salt and pepper to taste. Cover and chill overnight, if desired.
Yield: 6 cups

Rigatoni
1 pound rigatoni pasta, cooked
2½ cups (10 ounces) shredded Havarti cheese
⅓ cup sliced kalamata olives
⅓ cup grated Parmesan cheese
Garnish: chopped fresh basil

▸ Combine cooked pasta and Tomato Sauce in a large bowl, tossing to blend. Add Havarti, tossing well. Spoon mixture into a greased 3-quart baking dish. Sprinkle with olives and Parmesan cheese.
▸ Bake at 375° for 30 minutes or until thoroughly heated. Garnish, if desired.
Yield: 6 to 8 servings

Capellini with Goat Cheese

A simple, but delicious summertime supper served with marinated tomato wedges

12 ounces capellini (angel hair pasta)
2 tablespoons butter
2 cups fresh basil leaves, finely chopped
½ cup olive oil
4 garlic cloves, finely minced
1 teaspoon salt
½ cup freshly grated Parmesan cheese
3 to 4 ounces goat cheese, crumbled
¼ to ½ cup toasted walnuts, coarsely chopped
Freshly grated Parmesan cheese
Garnishes: thinly sliced prosciutto, freshly ground pepper, toasted walnuts, basil leaves

▸ Cook pasta according to package directions; drain, leaving ¼ cup liquid in Dutch oven.
▸ Add butter to pasta liquid; return pasta to pan and toss to coat.
▸ Combine basil, oil, garlic, salt, Parmesan cheese, goat cheese, and chopped walnuts; pour over pasta and toss to coat.
▸ Serve with additional Parmesan cheese and garnish, if desired.
Yield: 4 servings

Pasta Con Broccoli

A rich, creamy sauce with mushrooms and broccoli

6 tablespoons butter, divided
1½ cups fresh mushrooms, thinly sliced
1 teaspoon minced garlic
1 pint half-and-half
¼ cup tomato sauce
¼ teaspoon salt
¼ teaspoon ground white pepper
1 (10-ounce) package chopped frozen broccoli, thawed
¾ cup freshly grated Parmesan cheese
10 ounces cavatelli pasta (short, narrow, ripple-edged shells), cooked

▸ Melt 3 tablespoons butter in a Dutch oven over medium-high heat; add mushrooms and garlic and sauté 3 minutes or until tender. Transfer mushrooms and garlic to a bowl.

▸ Melt remaining 3 tablespoons butter in Dutch oven over medium heat; add half-and-half and tomato sauce and bring to a boil. Reduce heat and simmer until sauce is reduced by one-third. Stir in salt and pepper.

▸ Add broccoli to tomato mixture and cook over medium heat 5 minutes or until tender. Reduce heat to low and stir in Parmesan cheese. Add cooked pasta, mushrooms, and garlic, tossing to coat; cook 5 minutes or until thoroughly heated.

Yield: 4 servings

The Mayor's Red Beans and Rice

Our mayor's version of this New Orleans specialty always gets rave reviews.

1 pound dried red beans
8 cups water
1 tablespoon Worcestershire sauce
1 tablespoon soy-based marinade
1 tablespoon lemon juice
½ pound ham steak
6 tablespoons olive oil, divided
2 cups chopped onion
1 green bell pepper, chopped
1 red bell pepper, chopped
4 garlic cloves, diced
1 tablespoon dried sweet basil
2 tablespoons chopped fresh parsley
3 cups shredded cooked chicken
2 tablespoons lemon pepper
Hot cooked rice

▸ Place beans in a large Dutch oven; cover with water 2 inches above beans. Soak 8 hours or overnight. Drain and rinse.
▸ Return beans to Dutch oven; add 8 cups water, Worcestershire sauce, marinade, and lemon juice. Bring to a boil. Cover, reduce heat, and simmer, stirring occasionally, 2 hours or until beans are soft.
▸ Cook ham steak in 2 tablespoons hot oil in a large heavy skillet over medium-high heat; reduce heat to low and cook until tender. Remove from heat and let cool. Shred cooled meat.
▸ Sauté onion, bell peppers, garlic, basil, and parsley in remaining 4 tablespoons hot oil in skillet over medium heat, stirring often, until tender.
▸ Add ham, chicken, lemon pepper, and sautéed vegetables to bean mixture; cook over low heat 1 hour, stirring every 15 minutes and adding chicken broth or water if necessary.
▸ Serve over rice with French bread.
Yield: 8 to 10 servings

Oriental Shrimp Salad

Try a variety of sprouts - it adds interest.

Oriental Dressing
½ cup peanut oil
3 tablespoons apple cider vinegar
2 tablespoons soy sauce
2 teaspoons grated fresh gingerroot
2 garlic cloves, chopped

▸ Combine all ingredients in a jar; cover tightly and shake vigorously. Chill.
Yield: about ¾ cup

Salad
1 cup fresh bean sprouts or alfalfa sprouts
1 pound medium-size fresh shrimp, cooked, peeled, and deveined
1 small green bell pepper, finely chopped
4 to 6 green onions, sliced diagonally
Mixed salad greens or shredded romaine lettuce (optional)

▸ Rinse sprouts and drain.
▸ Combine sprouts, shrimp, bell pepper, and green onions in a bowl; chill
until ready to serve.
▸ When ready to serve, pour desired amount of Oriental Dressing over shrimp
mixture and toss to coat. Serve over salad greens, if desired.
Yield: 4 servings

Greek Salad

A salad-lover's feast with a few surprises

Potato Salad
2 pounds medium-size potatoes
1 cup finely chopped sweet onion
3 tablespoons red wine vinegar
¾ to 1 cup mayonnaise
1 teaspoon salt

▸ Cook potatoes in boiling water to cover Dutch oven 25 to 30 minutes or until tender; drain and let cool to touch. Peel and cut into ¾-inch cubes; place in a large bowl.
▸ Combine onion and vinegar in a small bowl; let stand 10 minutes. Stir in mayonnaise and salt. Pour mixture over potato and toss gently. Cover and chill.
Yield: about 6 cup

Greek Vinaigrette
¾ cup olive oil
¼ cup red wine vinegar
2 teaspoons dry mustard
1 teaspoon dried oregano

▸ Combine all ingredients in a jar; cover tightly and shake vigorously.
Yield: 1 cup

Salad
1 medium head leaf lettuce
3 tomatoes, cut into wedges
2 cucumbers, peeled and cut into spears
½ cup feta cheese
2 pounds medium-size fresh shrimp, cooked, peeled, and deveined
2 avocados, seeded, peeled, and cut into thin wedges
1 green bell pepper, cut into rings
1 red bell pepper, cut into rings
1 (16-ounce) jar sliced beets, drained
12 pitted ripe olives
8 radishes
6 to 8 pepperoncini salad peppers

▸ Line a 14-inch platter with lettuce leaves. Spoon Potato Salad into center of lettuce.
▸ Arrange tomato and cucumber alternately around edges of platter; sprinkle with cheese. Top with shrimp, avocado, bell peppers, beets, olives, radishes, and salad peppers.
▸ Drizzle desired amount of Greek Vinaigrette over salad and serve immediately.
Yield: 10 servings

Accompaniments

Etowah Youth Orchestras

One night a week, 60 young musicians from Etowah County high schools gather at the Center to practice. They can be heard laughing, blowing bubbles and sharing gossip until the Etowah Youth Symphony Orchestra's maestro taps the stand.

The laughing stops. They pick up their instruments and begin to play, producing a sound that impresses the most discriminating ear.

The Etowah Youth Symphony Orchestra is one of four ensembles that make up the Etowah Youth Orchestras. The Etowah Symphonic Wind Ensemble features the instrumentation of a concert band, the EYS Honor Strings is a chamber ensemble composed of the EYSO's top strings players, and the June Bugg Prelude Strings is the program's intermediate string orchestra.

How did this begin?

In 1991, an initiative by the late state legislator June Bugg led to the founding of the Etowah Youth Orchestras, which are administered by the Center for Cultural Arts. The program has garnered many awards including rankings among the top three youth orchestras in the country for the programming of new music by the American Society for Composers, Authors and Publishers each year from 1996 to 1999.

EYO teachers also offer strings instruction to students in six area elementary and middle schools. Together, the ensembles and the beginning orchestra program serve more than 250 students.

Participation in the EYO program gives young musicians an opportunity to play never-before-heard music, perform in major concerts, be heard on compact discs and perform in places like the Lincoln Center in New York and the Kennedy Center in Washington, D.C.

Roasted Asparagus

This is the best recipe for tender, crisp asparagus.

1 pound asparagus
1 tablespoon olive oil
½ teaspoon salt
⅛ teaspoon ground pepper
Grated rind and juice of 1 lemon

- Snap off tough ends of asparagus; remove scales with a knife or vegetable peeler, if desired.
- Place asparagus spears in a 15 x 10-inch jelly-roll pan; drizzle with oil and sprinkle with salt and pepper. Toss to coat.
- Bake at 400° for 10 to 15 minutes or until tender. Watch closely. Time will vary depending on size of asparagus. Remove from oven. Combine lemon rind and juice and drizzle over asparagus; toss to coat.

Yield: 3 to 4 servings

Guacamole

Great as a snack while you prepare tacos

1 ripe avocado
1 teaspoon minced onion
1 teaspoon olive oil
⅛ teaspoon salt
1 teaspoon lemon juice
Dash of pepper
Corn chips

- Slice avocado in half and remove pit. Scoop out pulp using a spoon. Mash pulp using a fork.
- Combine avocado pulp, onion, oil, salt, lemon juice, and pepper in a bowl, stirring with a fork until blended.
- Serve with corn chips.

Yield: 2 servings

Stuffed Broiled Avocados

Delicious served with Flank Steak with Horseradish Cream (see page 103) or Wayne's Smoked Lemon Chicken (see page 119).

2 tablespoons sliced green onions
1 tablespoon olive oil
1 (14.5-ounce) can diced tomatoes, drained
¼ cup soft breadcrumbs, divided
¼ cup grated fresh Parmesan cheese
3 ripe avocados, unpeeled
1 tablespoon butter or margarine, melted
¼ teaspoon salt
¼ teaspoon pepper

▶ Sauté green onions in hot oil in a skillet over medium heat until tender; add tomatoes. Reduce heat and simmer, stirring occasionally, 5 minutes. Add 2 tablespoons breadcrumbs, stirring well. Set aside.
▶ Combine remaining breadcrumbs and Parmesan cheese, stirring well.
▶ Cut avocados in half lengthwise; remove and discard seeds. Brush with melted butter and sprinkle with salt and pepper.
▶ Spoon tomato mixture evenly into avocado halves; sprinkle with cheese mixture.
▶ Broil 5 inches from heat 2 minutes or until cheese is melted.
Yield: 6 servings

Savory Green Beans

A tasty, low-fat way to cook green beans without salt pork or bacon drippings.

2 tablespoons chopped onion
1 garlic clove, minced
1 tablespoon olive oil
2 pounds fresh green beans, broken into 1½-inch pieces
1½ cups water
½ teaspoon sugar
1 teaspoon dried whole basil
½ teaspoon salt
¼ teaspoon pepper

▶ Sauté onion and garlic in hot oil in a large saucepan over medium heat.
▶ Add beans, water, sugar, basil, salt and pepper; bring to a boil. Cover, reduce heat, and simmer 25 minutes or until beans are tender.
Yield: 6 to 8 servings

Jessica's Sesame Green Beans

A favorite for cocktail suppers

2 pounds young, thin green beans
1 teaspoon salt, divided
¼ cup sesame seeds
¼ cup extra-virgin olive oil
2 tablespoons lemon juice
2 garlic cloves, minced
1 teaspoon crushed red pepper
Freshly ground black pepper

- Stem beans keeping the tender young green tips attached.
- Bring a Dutch oven full of water and ½ teaspoon salt to a boil; add beans and cook 3 to 4 minutes or until crisp-tender. Drain and rinse with cold water; drain again.
- Place a small dry skillet over medium heat until hot; add sesame seeds and cook, stirring constantly, 5 minutes or until golden brown.
- Combine oil, lemon juice, garlic, red pepper, black pepper, and remaining ½ teaspoon salt in a jar; cover tightly and shake vigorously.
- Transfer beans to a large serving bowl; sprinkle with sesame seeds. Drizzle with desired amount of dressing and toss to coat. Serve at room temperature.

Yield: 8 servings

Honey Glazed Carrots

These add color and a touch of sweetness to any menu.

1½ cups boiling water
1 pound carrots, scraped and cut into 3-inch long thin strips
2 tablespoons butter
2 tablespoons brown sugar
2 tablespoons honey
Chopped fresh parsley

- Combine water and carrots in a medium saucepan. Cook 8 to 10 minutes or until crisp-tender; drain and set aside.
- Melt butter in saucepan over low heat; add sugar and honey. Cook, stirring constantly, until sugar dissolves. Add carrots, gently stir to glaze and cook until thoroughly heated.
- Sprinkle with parsley and serve.

Yield: 3 to 4 servings

Great Greens

For a Dixie down-home dinner, serve with The Best Southern Fried Chicken (see page 113), Sweet Potato Crunch (see page 144), Marsue's Creamy Coleslaw (see page 76), and, of course, Neno's Cornbread (see page 155).

1 ham hock
6 pounds greens (mustard, collard, turnip, kale, or spinach)
4 ounces sliced salt pork, cut into 2-inch pieces
2 tablespoons vegetable oil
3 medium onions, quartered and thinly sliced
1 tablespoon chopped garlic
1 teaspoon salt
¾ teaspoon ground red pepper
¾ teaspoon freshly ground black pepper
1 (12-ounce) can beer
¼ cup distilled white vinegar
1 tablespoon molasses

▸ Bring ham hock to a boil in water to cover in a large saucepan; reduce heat to medium and cook 2 hours or until meat begins to separate from bone. Drain, reserving ham hock and cooking liquid. Cut meat from ham hock and discard fat; set meat aside.

▸ Wash greens and pick over; remove stems and set aside.

▸ Cook salt pork in hot oil in a Dutch oven over medium heat until crisp; drain on paper towels, reserving 3 tablespoons drippings in Dutch oven.

▸ Add onion to hot drippings and sauté over medium heat, stirring occasionally, 10 to 15 minutes or until golden.

▸ Add garlic, salt, red pepper, and black pepper to onion and cook 2 minutes. Add beer, vinegar, and molasses, stirring well.

▸ Gradually add greens to molasses mixture, one-third at a time, pressing down as they cook and wilt.

▸ Add ham, salt pork, and 2 to 3 cups ham hock liquid to greens; cook over medium heat, stirring often, 1 hour or until greens are tender. Add additional ham hock liquid, if desired.

Yield: 8 servings

NOTE: *For rich pork flavor and less fat, cook ham hock a day in advance. Remove ham hock, cover and refrigerate. Chill ham hock liquid for 8 hours or overnight and skim fat that rises to the top.*

Hoppin' John Black-Eyed Peas

Eating Hoppin' John is a New Year's tradition - good vittles and good luck. Try this flavorful way to cook black-eyed peas, without the ham and rice, any time of year.

3 bacon slices, quartered
1 cup thinly sliced celery
⅔ cup chopped onion
3 cups water
1 (16-ounce) package frozen black-eyed peas
1 tablespoon chicken flavored bouillon granules
¼ teaspoon crushed red pepper
1 bay leaf
¼ pound cooked ham, cut into ¼-inch cubes (optional)
Hot cooked rice (optional)

▸ Cook bacon in a Dutch oven over medium heat until crisp; remove from Dutch oven and drain on paper towels, reserving drippings. Crumble bacon and set aside.
▸ Sauté celery and onion in hot drippings in Dutch oven over medium heat until tender.
▸ Add 3 cups water, peas, bouillon, pepper, bay leaf, and, if desired, ham to Dutch oven and bring to a boil; cover, reduce heat, and simmer 40 to 45 minutes or until peas are tender.
▸ Remove and discard bay leaf. Serve over hot cooked rice, if desired, and top with crumbled bacon.
Yield: 6 to 8 servings

Sweet Onion Pie

It's yummy! Serve with pork roast, grilled chicken or beef.

½ cup butter or margarine
5 medium-size sweet onions, quartered and thinly sliced (about 6 cups)
3 large eggs, lightly beaten
¼ teaspoon salt
¼ teaspoon freshly ground pepper
2 drops pepper sauce
¼ teaspoon dry mustard
1 cup sour cream
1 unbaked 9-inch deep-dish pastry shell
½ cup (2 ounces) shredded sharp cheddar cheese

▸ Melt butter in a large skillet over medium-high heat; add onions and sauté 10 to 15 minutes or until liquid is evaporated and onions are translucent.
▸ Combine eggs, salt, pepper, pepper sauce, and mustard in a large bowl; add sour cream, stirring well. Add onions, stirring well.
▸ Pour egg mixture into piecrust and sprinkle with cheese.
▸ Bake at 450° for 20 minutes. Reduce oven temperature to 325° and bake 20 more minutes or until top is golden brown.
▸ Remove from oven and let cool on a wire rack 10 minutes. Serve warm or at room temperature.
Yield: 1 (9-inch) deep-dish pie

Balsamic Potatoes

It's delicious hot or cold and great for picnics or dinner.

2 pounds red potatoes, unpeeled and cubed (about 6 cups)
⅓ cup chopped fresh parsley
1 to 2 garlic cloves, minced
¼ cup olive oil
1 tablespoon balsamic vinegar
1 teaspoon salt
Garnish: fresh parsley

▸ Cook potatoes in boiling salted water to cover in a Dutch oven 8 to 10 minutes or until tender. Drain and return to Dutch oven.
▸ Combine parsley, garlic, oil, vinegar, and salt, stirring well; pour over potatoes, tossing to coat.
▸ Serve immediately or chill and serve cold. Garnish, if desired.
Yield: 6 servings

Potato Gratin with Boursin

Boursin, a buttery cream cheese flavored with herbs, garlic and black pepper, lends a delectable, rich flavor.

2 cups heavy cream
1 (5-ounce) package Boursin cheese or ½ cup of Boursin Cheese (see page 51)
½ teaspoon salt
½ teaspoon pepper
3 pounds red potatoes, unpeeled and cut into ⅛-inch slices
1½ tablespoons chopped fresh parsley

- Cook first 4 ingredients in a medium saucepan over low heat, stirring constantly, until cheese melts.
- Layer half of potato slices in a greased 13 x 9 x 2-inch baking dish; top with half of cream mixture, spreading to cover. Repeat layers.
- Bake at 350° for 1 hour or until bubbly and top is golden brown.
- Remove from oven and sprinkle with parsley.

Yield: 8 to 10 servings

Garlic Mashed Potatoes

Medium-size round potatoes, referred to as boiling potatoes, are best for mashing. Yukon gold, round potatoes with yellow to golden skins, have a moist succulent texture and make excellent mashed potatoes.

2 pounds Yukon gold or russet potatoes, peeled and cut into 2-inch cubes
2 garlic cloves, peeled and halved
2 tablespoons salt
⅓ cup buttermilk
¼ cup cream
Salt
Freshly ground pepper

- Cook potatoes, garlic, and 2 tablespoons salt in water to cover in a Dutch oven over high heat. Bring to a boil and cook 15 to 20 minutes or until tender when pierced with a fork. Drain, reserving liquid.
- Return potatoes and garlic to Dutch oven and mash with a potato masher, leaving slightly lumpy. Add buttermilk, cream, salt, and pepper to taste, stirring gently with a spoon. Add reserved potato liquid to desired consistency.

Yield: 4 servings

Cheesy Mashed Potato Casserole

For the best mashed potatoes, lightly mix; overbeating will make them sticky and starchy.

6 medium russet potatoes, peeled and quartered (about 2 ½ pounds)
1 tablespoon salt
2 tablespoons butter or margarine
¼ cup chopped onion
1 to 3 garlic cloves, minced
½ cup milk
1 cup (4 ounces) shredded sharp cheddar cheese
1 (8-ounce) container sour cream
1 teaspoon salt
¼ teaspoon pepper

▸ Combine potatoes, 1 tablespoon salt and water to cover in a Dutch oven over high heat. Bring to a boil, reduce heat and simmer 20 minutes or until tender when pierced with a fork. Drain.
▸ Melt butter in a Dutch oven over medium heat; add onion and garlic and sauté until tender.
▸ Beat potatoes at medium speed with an electric mixer just until smooth. Add onion, garlic, milk, cheese, sour cream, salt, and pepper, beating just until combined.
▸ Pour potato mixture in a 2-quart baking dish coated with vegetable cooking spray.
▸ Bake at 350° for 30 minutes or until thoroughly heated.
Yield: 6 servings

Roasted Vegetable Casserole

Lightly seasoned with herbs and olive oil for a healthy side dish

2 pounds potatoes, peeled and thinly sliced (about 6 cups)
1 large red, yellow, or green bell pepper, cut into strips
1 medium onion, quartered and thinly sliced
1 cup thinly sliced celery
2 cups thinly sliced carrot
3 small zucchini, unpeeled and thinly sliced (about 2 cups)
⅓ cup olive oil
1 to 1½ teaspoons dried Italian herb seasoning
1½ teaspoons salt
1 teaspoon pepper

3 large ripe tomatoes, sliced
Olive oil cooking spray
Freshly grated Parmesan cheese (optional)

▸ Combine first 6 ingredients in a large heavy-duty zip-top plastic bag; add oil, Italian seasoning, salt, and pepper. Seal bag and toss to coat.
▸ Coat a 13 x 9 x 2-inch casserole with cooking spray. Place vegetables in casserole, arrange tomato slices on top. Coat generously with olive oil cooking spray.
▸ Bake at 350° for 1 hour and 15 minutes to 1 hour and 30 minutes or until potatoes and carrots are tender.
▸ Sprinkle with cheese during last 10 minutes of baking, if desired.
Yield: 8 servings
NOTE: All the vegetables, except potatoes, may be sliced a day in advance. Place in large heavy-duty zip-top plastic bag and refrigerate. To bake, add potatoes and proceed as directed.

Spicy Scalloped Potatoes

Rich nutty Gruyère and crushed red pepper lend a zesty flavor.

2 tablespoons butter
1 garlic clove, minced
1 shallot, chopped
½ teaspoon crushed red pepper
1¼ cups milk
2 cups whipping cream
½ teaspoon salt
¼ teaspoon freshly ground black pepper
2½ pounds red potatoes, unpeeled and cut into ½-inch slices
1½ cups (6 ounces) shredded Gruyère or Swiss cheese
½ cup freshly grated Parmesan cheese

▸ Melt butter in a Dutch oven over medium heat; add garlic, shallot, and red pepper and sauté 2 minutes.
▸ Add milk, cream, salt, and black pepper to Dutch oven, stirring well. Add potatoes and bring to a boil over medium heat. Reduce heat and simmer, stirring occasionally, 5 minutes.
▸ Spoon half of potato mixture into a greased 12 x 8 x 2-inch baking dish. Sprinkle with half of cheeses. Repeat layers.
▸ Bake at 350° for 45 to 60 minutes or until bubbly and top is golden brown. Let stand at room temperature 30 minutes before serving.
Yield: 8 servings
NOTE: To make ahead, cover and refrigerate assembled casserole. Let stand at room temperature for 1 hour before baking. Bake as directed.

Sweet Potato Crunch

"This is my Gran's recipe. She made it every Thanksgiving of my life."

2½ pounds sweet potatoes, unpeeled
½ to 1 cup sugar
⅔ cup butter, divided and softened
2 large eggs, lightly beaten
⅓ cup milk
1 teaspoon vanilla extract
½ to 1 cup firmly packed light brown sugar
⅓ cup all-purpose flour
1 cup chopped pecans
1 cup flaked coconut (optional)

▸ Cook potatoes in boiling water to cover in a large Dutch oven 30 minutes or until tender; drain. Let potatoes cool slightly. Peel and cut into chunks.
▸ Beat potatoes, ⅓ cup butter, eggs, milk, and vanilla at medium speed with an electric mixer until smooth.
▸ Spoon mixture into a greased 12 x 8 x 2-inch baking dish.
▸ Combine remaining ⅓ cup butter, brown sugar, flour, pecans, and, if desired, coconut, stirring until crumbly. Sprinkle over potato mixture.
▸ Bake at 350° for 30 minutes or until thoroughly heated and topping is lightly browned.
Yield: 6 servings

Apricot-Glazed Sweet Potatoes

Just enough sweetness to enhance yummy yams. You can also use the sauce to bake apples or pears.

3 pounds sweet potatoes, unpeeled
½ cup firmly packed brown sugar
1½ tablespoons cornstarch
¼ teaspoon salt
⅛ teaspoon ground cinnamon
1 cup apricot nectar
½ cup water
2 tablespoons butter or margarine
½ cup chopped pecans

▸ Cook sweet potatoes in boiling salted water to cover in a Dutch oven 30 minutes or until tender. Drain and let cool to touch. Peel and cut into ⅓-inch

slices. Arrange slices in a shallow 2-quart baking dish.
- Combine brown sugar, cornstarch, salt, and cinnamon in a saucepan, stirring well; add nectar and ⅓ cup water. Cook over medium heat, stirring constantly, until thickened and bubbly.
- Stir in butter and pecans and pour over sweet potato slices.
- Bake at 350° for 30 to 40 minutes or until bubbly.

Yield: about 6 servings

Spanakopita

For a lower-fat version of this traditional Greek spinach pie, generously spray the phyllo pastry with butter-flavored cooking spray rather than using melted butter.

3 pounds fresh spinach
8 green onions, finely chopped
⅓ cup extra-virgin olive oil
¾ cup pine nuts
1 pound feta cheese, crumbled
Grated nutmeg, to taste
Salt and freshly ground pepper to taste
12 phyllo pastry sheets
½ cup unsalted butter, melted

- Remove stems from spinach and wash thoroughly. Cook spinach, covered, in a large Dutch oven over medium heat 3 to 5 minutes or until wilted. (Do not add water, the water clinging to leaves after washing will steam the spinach.) Drain well in a sieve, pressing with back of spoon.
- Sauté green onions in hot oil in Dutch oven over medium heat until tender. Add spinach, pine nuts, feta, nutmeg, and salt and pepper to taste, stirring well. Set mixture aside.
- Trim phyllo sheets to fit a 13 x 9 x 2-inch baking dish; brush each of 4 sheets with melted butter or spray generously with butter-flavored vegetable cooking spray and layer in baking dish.
- Spoon half of spinach mixture over phyllo sheets in baking dish. Brush 4 more phyllo sheets with butter and place over spinach. Repeat layers ending with phyllo sheets. Brush top with butter. Chill until ready to cook.
- Bake at 350° for 35 to 45 minutes or until golden brown.
- Cut into squares and serve hot or at room temperature.

Yield: 8 to 10 servings

NOTE: *Two (10-ounce) packages frozen chopped spinach, thawed, but not cooked, may be substituted for fresh spinach. Drain well in a sieve, pressing with back of spoon to remove moisture, chop coarsely. Proceed as directed above.*

Mushrooms Florentine

Even people who don't like spinach enjoy this recipe.

4 tablespoons butter or margarine, divided
1 pound fresh mushrooms, sliced
½ teaspoon garlic salt
¼ cup chopped onion
1 teaspoon salt
2 (10-ounce) packages frozen chopped spinach, thawed and well drained
2 cups (8 ounces) shredded sharp cheddar cheese, divided

▸ Melt 2 tablespoons butter in a skillet over medium-high heat; add mushrooms and sauté until tender. Remove from skillet and sprinkle with garlic salt.
▸ Melt remaining 2 tablespoons butter in skillet over medium heat; add onion and sauté until translucent. Sprinkle with salt. Add spinach, stirring well.
▸ Place spinach mixture in a 2-quart baking dish. Sprinkle with half of cheese. Top with mushroom mixture and remaining cheese.
▸ Bake at 350° for 20 minutes or until thoroughly heated.
Yield: 8 servings

Summer Squash

Sour cream lends a tangy flavor and creamy texture.

2 to 2½ pounds yellow squash, cut into ½-inch slices
½ cup sour cream
2 to 4 tablespoons butter or margarine, melted
2 green onions, minced
1 teaspoon salt
Dash of pepper
½ cup soft breadcrumbs
1 tablespoon butter, melted
¼ cup freshly grated Parmesan cheese (optional)

▸ Cook squash in boiling water to cover in a saucepan 5 to 7 minutes or until tender; drain.
▸ Combine squash, sour cream, 2 to 4 tablespoons melted butter, green onions, salt, and pepper; spoon into a greased 2-quart baking dish.
▸ Combine breadcrumbs, 1 tablespoon melted butter, and cheese, stirring well. Sprinkle over squash mixture.
▸ Bake at 350° for 25 minutes or until bubbly.
Yield: 8 to 10 servings

Squash Casserole Supreme

A melange of tasty textures

1 pound yellow squash, sliced
1 teaspoon salt
1 teaspoon sugar
½ cup chopped onion
¼ cup butter or margarine
½ cup mayonnaise
½ cup sliced water chestnuts
½ cup chopped bell pepper
1 large egg, lightly beaten
½ cup (2 ounces) shredded cheddar cheese
1 cup crushed buttery crackers, (about 36 crackers)

▸ Combine squash, salt, sugar, and water to cover. Bring to a boil, reduce heat and simmer 8 to 10 minutes or until tender. Drain and mash.
▸ Combine mashed squash, onion, butter, mayonnaise, water chestnuts, bell pepper, egg, and cheese, stirring well.
▸ Spoon squash mixture into a greased 1½-quart baking dish. Sprinkle with cracker crumbs.
▸ Bake at 350° for 30 minutes or until bubbly.

Yield: 4 to 6 servings
NOTE: Recipe may be doubled and baked in a greased 3-quart baking dish.

Herb-Baked Squash

How can anything this easy be so good?

4 small yellow squash or zucchini (about 1⅓ pounds)
1 tablespoon melted butter or olive oil
Salt and pepper to taste
½ teaspoon crushed rosemary
⅛ teaspoon sage
3 tablespoons fresh grated Parmesan cheese

▸ Cut squash in half lengthwise. Place, cut side up, in a lightly greased 12 x 8 x 2-inch baking dish. Drizzle with butter and sprinkle with salt and pepper to taste.
▸ Combine rosemary and sage, sprinkle over squash. Sprinkle with cheese.
▸ Bake at 400° for 20 to 25 minutes or until crisp-tender.

Yield: 4 servings

Tomato, Cheese, and Herb Tart

An impressive presentation - serve with a tossed salad for a light summer supper.

Tart Crust

1¼ cups all-purpose flour
¼ teaspoon salt
½ cup unsalted butter, chilled and cut into pieces
3 to 4 tablespoons ice water

▸ Process first 3 ingredients in a food processor until mixture resembles coarse meal. Add water, 1 tablespoon at a time, processing after each addition until moist clumps form. Gather dough into a ball and flatten into a disk. Wrap in plastic wrap and chill 30 minutes.
▸ Roll dough into a 13-inch round on a lightly floured surface. Transfer to an 11-inch tart pan with removable bottom. Trim edges. Freeze 15 minutes.
▸ Line crust with aluminum foil and fill with dried beans or pie weights.
▸ Bake at 375° for 15 minutes or until crust is set. Remove foil and beans and bake 15 more minutes or until crust is pale golden.
▸ Place on a wire rack and let cool. Cover and let stand at room temperature up to 1 day.

Filling

5 medium tomatoes, cut into ½-inch thick slices
9 ounces Emmentaler or Gruyère cheese, thinly sliced
1 tablespoon minced fresh basil or 1 teaspoon dried
1 teaspoon minced fresh thyme or ¼ teaspoon dried
1 teaspoon minced fresh oregano or ¼ teaspoon dried
3 tablespoons freshly grated Parmesan cheese
Ground pepper to taste
Garnishes: fresh basil, oregano, and thyme

▸ Place tomato slices on paper towels. Let drain 45 minutes.
▸ Top crust with cheese slices. Arrange tomato slices on cheese, starting at outer edge of crust, slightly overlapping slices.
▸ Sprinkle tomato slices with herbs and Parmesan cheese. Season with pepper to taste.
▸ Bake at 375° for 35 minutes or until cheese is melted and tomato is tender. Place on a wire rack and let cool slightly.
▸ Remove tart pan sides and cut into wedges to serve.
Yield: 8 servings

Corn-Zucchini-Tomato Sauté

Nice, fresh vegetable medley, that's great with grilled chicken or steaks.

1½ tablespoons margarine or olive oil
2 cups fresh corn kernels (about 3 ears) or frozen corn kernels, thawed
1 medium zucchini, trimmed and thinly sliced (2 cups)
½ cup sliced green onions
¼ cup chopped green bell pepper
1 cup peeled and chopped tomato
1 tablespoon chopped fresh or 1 teaspoon dried basil
1 tablespoon chopped fresh or 1 teaspoon dried oregano
1 teaspoon sugar
¼ teaspoon salt
¼ teaspoon lemon pepper
¼ cup freshly grated Parmesan cheese

▸ Melt margarine in a large skillet over medium-high heat; add corn, zucchini, green onions, and bell pepper. Sauté 5 to 8 minutes or until crisp-tender.

▸ Add tomato, basil, oregano, sugar, salt, and lemon pepper to skillet and cook, stirring constantly, over medium heat 3 minutes or until vegetables are tender.

▸ Sprinkle with cheese, if desired, and serve immediately.

Yield: 6 servings

Cheesy Tomato Pie

An easy crust and lots of cheese makes this a winner for summer tomatoes.

Biscuit Mix Pie Crust
1 cup biscuit mix
¼ cup butter or margarine, softened
2 tablespoons boiling water

▸ Combine biscuit mix and butter in a bowl, stirring with a fork until crumbly. Add 2 tablespoons boiling water, stirring well.
▸ Press soft dough into a 9-inch pie plate using floured fingers.
▸ Bake at 350° for 10 minutes or until set. Place on a wire rack and let cool completely.

Filling
3 medium tomatoes, peeled and cut into ½-inch slices
2 cups (8 ounces) shredded sharp cheddar cheese or Monterey Jack, divided
Salt and pepper to taste
2 tablespoons chopped fresh basil or 1 teaspoon dried Italian seasoning
3 tablespoons finely chopped onions
½ cup mayonnaise

▸ Place tomato slices on paper towels and let drain 45 minutes.
▸ Sprinkle 1 cup cheese on crust.
▸ Arrange tomato slices on cheese, starting at outer edge of crust, slightly overlapping slices. Repeat in center. Sprinkle with salt and pepper to taste, basil, and onions.
▸ Combine mayonnaise and remaining cheese; spread over tomato slices.
▸ Bake at 325° on lowest oven rack 45 to 60 minutes or until firm and lightly browned.
Yield: 1 (9-inch) pie

Tomato-Zucchini Gratin

This colorful dish is as pleasing to the palate as it is to the eye.

3 medium zucchini, thinly sliced (1½ pounds)
4 medium-size ripe tomatoes, peeled and thinly sliced (2 pounds)
¾ cup grated Parmesan cheese, divided
2 garlic cloves, minced
1 teaspoon dried thyme
¼ teaspoon salt
¼ teaspoon pepper
2 tablespoons olive oil

▸ Arrange half of zucchini slices in the bottom of a greased 8-inch square baking dish; top with half of tomato slices. Sprinkle with ¼ cup cheese.
▸ Combine garlic, thyme, salt, and pepper; sprinkle half over vegetables and cheese in baking dish.
▸ Top with remaining zucchini and tomatoes; sprinkle with remaining herb mixture. Drizzle with oil and sprinkle with remaining ½ cup Parmesan cheese.
▸ Bake at 400° for 20 to 25 minutes. Serve with a slotted spoon.
Yield: 6 servings

Wild Rice Casserole

A versatile dish that suits almost any meat or seafood

1 (6-ounce) package long-grain and wild rice mix with herbs
  and seasonings
¼ cup butter or margarine
1 cup chopped onion
¼ cup sherry

▸ Cook rice according to package directions.
▸ Melt butter in a small skillet over medium heat; add onion and sauté until tender.
▸ Combine hot cooked rice, onion, and sherry; spoon into a greased 8-inch square baking dish.
▸ Bake at 350° for 20 minutes or until thoroughly heated.
Yield: 4 servings

Risotto

Arborio is an Italian-grown rice that's shorter and fatter than other short grain rice. The high-starch grain lends a creamy texture to risotto.

6 to 8 cups chicken or veal stock (Easy Chicken Stock, see page 96)
½ cup finely chopped shallots
3 tablespoons olive oil
1 cup Arborio rice
½ cup white wine
4 to 6 tablespoons butter
½ cup grated Parmesan cheese
¼ cup chopped parsley
Salt and freshly ground pepper to taste
Garnish: shaved Parmesan cheese

▸ Bring chicken stock to a boil in a large saucepan; reduce heat and simmer.
▸ Sauté shallots in hot oil in a large heavy saucepan over medium-high heat 5 minutes or until translucent. Add rice and cook, stirring constantly, 3 to 4 minutes or until rice begins to make a clicking sound like glass beads. Reduce heat to medium.
▸ Add wine to rice mixture and cook, stirring constantly, until wine is absorbed.
▸ Add ¾ cup hot stock to rice mixture, gently stirring constantly until liquid is absorbed. Repeat procedure with remaining stock mixture, ¾ cup at a time. Rice should be al dente. (Cooking time is about 20 to 30 minutes.)
▸ Remove from heat and stir in butter, cheese, parsley, and salt and pepper to taste. Garnish, if desired.
Yield: 4 servings

Baked Rice

Always a good substitute for potatoes.

¼ cup butter or margarine, melted
1¼ cups uncooked long-grain rice
1 (10½-ounce) can condensed beef consommé, undiluted
1 (10½-ounce) can condensed French onion soup, undiluted
1 or 2 (4-ounce) cans sliced mushrooms, drained (optional)

▸ Combine first 4 ingredients and, if desired, mushrooms in an ungreased 2-quart baking dish.
▸ Bake, covered, at 350° for 50 to 60 minutes or until rice is tender.
Yield: 5 servings

Polenta

Serve Polenta, an Italian cornmeal specialty, instead of grits, rice, or potatoes.

2 cups water
½ teaspoon salt
⅔ cup yellow cornmeal
¼ cup freshly grated Romano cheese
1 tablespoon butter
¼ cup chopped fresh basil (optional)
Ground pepper to taste

▸ Bring 2 cups water and salt to a boil in a heavy saucepan. Gradually whisk in cornmeal. Reduce heat to medium-low and simmer, whisking constantly, 6 minutes or until polenta is thickened. Remove from heat.
▸ Add cheese and butter, whisking until melted. Stir in basil, if desired. Season generously with pepper.

Yield: 4 servings

NOTE: For baked polenta, spoon cooked polenta into 8 x 8 x 2-inch pan. Chill until cold, about 1 hour (or a day in advance). Cut polenta into squares and place on greased baking sheet. Bake at 350° for 10 to 12 minutes or until hot. Serve with salsa, if desired.

Savory Butter Sauce

Cornstarch creates satiny, clear sauces. For best results stir gently and cook only 1 minute after mixture comes to a boil over medium heat.

⅓ cup sliced almonds
½ cup butter
1 chicken bouillon cube, crumbled
1 tablespoon cornstarch
½ cup cold water
⅓ cup sliced green onions

▸ Bake almonds in a shallow pan at 350°, stirring once, 5 to 10 minutes or until toasted.
▸ Melt butter in a saucepan over medium heat; add bouillon, stirring well.
▸ Combine cornstarch and ½ cup cold water, stirring to dissolve; gradually add to butter mixture, stirring gently.
▸ Add green onions and toasted almonds, stirring gently. Bring to a boil and cook 1 minute.
▸ Serve over broccoli, cauliflower, asparagus, green beans, or peas.

Yield: about 1 cup

Lemon Sauce

This luscious sauce is great over a variety of vegetables. The water prevents the butter from separating.

Grated rind of 1 lemon
3 tablespoons fresh lemon juice
¼ cup water
5 tablespoons butter, cut into 5 pieces
Salt and freshly ground pepper to taste

▸ Bring first 3 ingredients to a boil in a 9-inch skillet over high heat; cook 1 minute or until mixture begins to thicken.
▸ Add butter, 1 tablespoon at a time, whisking constantly until butter melts. Season with salt and pepper to taste.
▸ Serve over your favorite vegetable.
Yield: about ¾ cup

Golden Cashew Butter

Browned butter, "beurre noisette," has a rich, nutty flavor that's delicious over fish as well as vegetables.

½ cup butter
¾ cup salted cashews (coarsely chopped, if desired)
1 tablespoon fresh lemon juice
½ cup thinly sliced green onions
2 tablespoons chopped fresh parsley

▸ Melt butter in a medium skillet over low heat; add cashews and cook, stirring occasionally, 5 minutes or until butter is a light golden brown and cashews are toasted (butter will be foamy).
▸ Remove from heat and stir in lemon juice, green onions, and parsley.
▸ Serve over fish or your favorite vegetable.
Yield: 1½ cups

Rising Stars

YouthAlive!

Patrons of art museums are usually adults who have grown to appreciate museums through a lifetime of exposure to the Arts. Children's museums are believed to be frequented exclusively by parents with small children. But thanks to a program called YouthALIVE!, teenagers have also found a home at the Center.

In 1991, with support from the DeWitt Wallace-Reader's Digest Fund, the Association of Science-Technology Centers (ASTC) began to encourage adolescent involvement in museums by launching YouthALIVE! (Youth Achievement through Learning, Involvement, Volunteering and Employment). The nationwide initiative was aimed at bringing opportunities for education and personal growth to youth.

Everyone can benefit from the knowledge and beauty that a museum or art center offers, but too often the last to be exposed to the world of the Arts are teenagers. Through YouthALIVE!, museums can reach out to teenagers and make a difference in their young lives.

In 1995, the YouthALIVE! program started at the Center for Cultural Arts.

The Center's staff now offers young people a constructive place to spend after-school and summer hours. By working as docents, demonstrators, science program presenters and birthday party workers, they are able to make connections between museum experiences, career possibilities and educational paths.

The ASTC program ended in 1999. But the YouthALIVE! program at the Center for Cultural Arts lives on. More than 75 students have graduated from the program and have been exposed to the workings of a museum, formed relationships with staff and discovered a fulfilling direction in life.

Whipping Cream Biscuits

For easy and delicious shortcakes, add 2 tablespoons sugar.

2 cups self-rising flour
1 cup whipping cream

▸ Combine flour and cream in a bowl, stirring with a fork until blended (dough will be stiff).
▸ Turn dough out on a lightly floured surface and knead 10 to 12 times.
▸ Roll dough to ½-inch thickness; cut with a 2-inch biscuit cutter. Place biscuits on a lightly greased baking sheet.
▸ Bake at 450° for 10 to 12 minutes or until lightly browned.

Yield: 1 dozen

Neno's Cornbread

"This is my grandmother's recipe, which I prefer, because it's made without an egg."

3 tablespoons bacon drippings or vegetable oil
1 cup cornmeal
⅛ teaspoon baking soda
2 teaspoons baking powder
¼ teaspoon salt
½ cup buttermilk
½ cup water

▸ Pour drippings into a 9 to 12-inch cast iron skillet; place in a 375° oven 5 minutes or until drippings are heated. Remove skillet from oven, tilting to coat sides with drippings.
▸ Combine cornmeal, baking soda, baking powder, and salt in a medium bowl, stirring to blend.
▸ Add buttermilk, ½ cup water, and hot drippings to cornmeal mixture, stirring just until dry ingredients are moistened.
▸ Pour batter into hot skillet.
▸ Place skillet in 375° oven and increase temperature to 450°. Cook 25 to 30 minutes or until top is browned and bread pulls away from edges.

Yield: 6 to 8 servings

Pan de Helate Cornbread

"This tastes just like the cornbread at our favorite catfish restaurant."

1 cup butter, softened
¼ cup sugar
4 large eggs
1 cup all-purpose flour
1 cup cornmeal
4 teaspoons baking powder
½ teaspoon salt
1 (4.5-ounce) can chopped green chiles
1 (14.5-ounce) can cream-style corn
½ cup (2 ounces) shredded Monterey Jack cheese
½ cup (2 ounces) shredded cheddar cheese

▸ Grease and flour a 12 x 8 x 2-inch baking dish.
▸ Beat butter and sugar at medium speed with an electric mixer until creamy; add eggs, beating after each addition.
▸ Combine flour, cornmeal, baking powder, and salt; add to creamed mixture, beating until blended. Stir in chiles, corn, and cheeses.
▸ Pour batter into prepared baking dish.
▸ Bake at 325° for 50 to 55 minutes or until a wooden pick inserted in center comes out clean. Serve warm.

Yield: 6 to 8 servings

Quick Homemade Dinner Rolls

Easy and just as good without the optional butter or cheese

2 cups self-rising flour
½ teaspoon sugar
¾ cup milk
¼ cup butter, melted
¼ cup mayonnaise
½ cup (2 ounces) shredded cheddar cheese (optional)
Melted butter (optional)

▸ Grease muffin pan.
▸ Combine first 5 ingredients and, if desired, cheese, in a large bowl, stirring to blend.
▸ Drop dough into muffin pan, using a spoon and filling each cup two-thirds full.
▸ Bake at 450° for 12 minutes or until lightly browned. Drizzle with melted butter, if desired.

Yield: about 1 dozen

Clara's Sally Lunn Bread

Luncheon guests will savor this rich, slightly sweet, cake-like bread. It's also good for strawberry shortcake and toasted for breakfast.

1 (¼-ounce) envelope active dry yeast
¼ cup warm water (105° to 115°)
¾ cup milk
¼ cup sugar
¼ cup shortening
½ teaspoon salt
1 large egg
2½ cups all-purpose flour

▸ Grease a 6-cup Bundt pan.
▸ Combine yeast and ¼ cup warm water in a 1-cup glass measuring cup; let stand 5 minutes.
▸ Cook milk, sugar, shortening, and salt in a saucepan over medium heat, stirring constantly, until shortening is melted. Remove from heat and let cool to 105° to 115°.
▸ Beat yeast mixture, milk mixture, and egg at medium speed with an electric mixer until well blended. Gradually add flour, beating at low speed until blended.
▸ Cover and let rise in a warm place (85°), free from drafts, 1 hour or until doubled in bulk. Stir dough down; cover and let rise in a warm place, free from drafts, 30 minutes or until doubled in bulk (dough will be very sticky).
▸ Stir dough down and spoon into greased Bundt pan. Cover and let rise in a warm place, free from drafts, 30 minutes or until doubled in bulk.
▸ Bake at 350° for 25 to 30 minutes. Remove from pan immediately and serve warm.
Yield: 1 loaf

Focaccia

Focaccia, an Italian yeast bread sprinkled with olive oil, salt, and herbs, is great for sandwiches, burgers, and as a pizza crust.

4 cups bread flour
1 teaspoon salt
1 (¼-ounce) envelope active dry yeast
½ teaspoon sugar
1¼ cups warm water (105° to 115°), divided
¼ cup olive oil
Dried oregano or rosemary

▸ Combine flour and salt in a large bowl. Set aside.
▸ Combine yeast, sugar, and ¾ cup warm water in a 1-cup glass measuring cup; let stand 10 minutes or until yeast is dissolved.
▸ Add yeast mixture, oil, and remaining ¾ cup water to flour mixture, stirring to form a soft dough and adding water if necessary.
▸ Transfer dough to a lightly floured surface and knead 5 minutes or until smooth and elastic.
▸ Place dough in a greased bowl, turning to grease top. Cover with a towel and let rise in a warm place (85°), free from drafts, 2 hours or until doubled in bulk.
▸ Transfer dough to a floured surface and knead 3 more minutes. Divide dough into 8 balls. Roll each ball to a 5 to 5½-inch circle on a floured surface. Place circles on 2 oiled baking sheets.
▸ Brush dough with oil and make indentations on surface using your finger tips. Sprinkle with herbs.
▸ Bake at 425° for 12 to 15 minutes or until golden brown.
Yield: 8 rounds

Sourdough Bread

A wonderful loaf bread with just a hint of the sourdough starter.

Sourdough Starter
2 cups bread flour
1 (¼-ounce) envelope active dry yeast
2 cups warm water (120° to 130°)

▸ Combine all ingredients in a large glass bowl, stirring well.
▸ Cover with plastic wrap and let stand in a warm place (85°), free from drafts, 12 to 24 hours.

Bread
1 cup Sourdough Starter
½ cup sugar
½ cup vegetable oil
1 tablespoon salt
1½ cups warm water (120° to 130°)
6 cups bread flour

▸ Combine all ingredients in a large bowl, stirring until a stiff dough forms.
▸ Divide dough into 3 portions. Place each portion in a large greased bowl, turning to grease tops. Cover each with a cloth and let rise in a warm place (85°), free from drafts, overnight.
▸ Punch dough down and knead each portion on a lightly floured surface 2 to 3 minutes.
▸ Shape each portion into a loaf and place in a greased 9 x 5 x 3-inch loaf pan. Spray lightly with oil. Cover and let rise in a warm place, free from drafts, several hours or until doubled in bulk.
▸ Bake at 350° for 30 to 35 minutes or until loaves sound hollow when tapped. Remove from pans and cool on wire racks.

Yield: 3 loaves

VARIATION: Sourdough Cinnamon Bread
⅓ recipe Sourdough Bread dough (after kneading and before shaping into loaves)
¼ cup butter, softened
¼ cup firmly packed brown sugar
1½ teaspoons ground cinnamon
¼ cup raisins (optional)
1 tablespoon butter, melted

▸ Grease a 9 x 5 x 3-inch loaf pan.
▸ Roll dough into a 12 x 9-inch rectangle and spread softened butter within ½ inch of edge. Sprinkle with brown sugar, cinnamon, and, if desired, raisins.
▸ Roll up dough, jelly roll fashion, starting with a short end. Turn ends under and place in greased loaf pan.
▸ Brush melted butter over top. Cover and let rise in a warm place (85°), free from drafts, 2 hours or until doubled in bulk.
▸ Bake at 350° for 30 to 35 minutes or until loaf sounds hollow when tapped. Remove from pan and let cool on a wire rack.

Yield: 1 loaf

Honey-Oatmeal Bread

What a wonderfully healthy way to start your day.

1½ cups water
½ cup honey
⅓ cup butter or margarine
5½ to 6½ cups all-purpose flour, divided
1 cup quick-cooking oats
2 teaspoons salt
2 (¼-ounce) packages active dry yeast
2 large eggs
1 tablespoon water
1 egg white
Quick-cooking oats

- Cook first 3 ingredients in a saucepan over medium-low heat, stirring constantly, until warm (120° to 130°).
- Combine 5 cups flour, oats, salt, and yeast in a large bowl; gradually add honey mixture and eggs, beating at low speed with a heavy-duty electric mixer 2 minutes or until blended.
- Gradually add remaining flour, ½ cup at a time, stirring to form a soft dough.
- Turn dough out on a well-floured surface and knead 10 minutes or until smooth and elastic. Transfer to a well-greased bowl, turning to grease top.
- Cover and let rise in a warm place (85°), free from drafts, 1 hour or until doubled in bulk.
- Punch dough down and let stand 15 minutes. Divide dough in half and shape each portion into a loaf. Place in 2 (8½ x 4½ x 2½-inch) greased loaf pans. Cover and let rise in a warm place, free from drafts, 1 hour or until doubled in bulk.
- Combine 1 tablespoon water and egg white, stirring well; brush over tops of loaves and sprinkle with oatmeal.
- Bake at 375° for 40 minutes or until loaves sound hollow when tapped, covering with aluminum foil after 25 minutes if necessary to prevent over browning. Remove from pans and let cool on wire racks.

Yield: 2 loaves

Traditional Rye Bread

A combination of dill seed and caraway seeds lends an authentic taste and bite.

Sponge
1 (¼-ounce) envelope active dry yeast
3 tablespoons light brown sugar
1 cup medium rye flour
2 cups warm water (120° to 130°)
1½ cups unbleached all-purpose flour

▸ Combine first 4 ingredients in a large bowl, stirring to blend; let stand 5 minutes.
▸ Add all-purpose flour to yeast mixture and beat at medium speed with an electric mixer 5 minutes or until creamy and well moistened.
▸ Cover and let stand at room temperature until bubbly (at least 4 hours or overnight).

Bread
Sponge
½ cup medium rye flour
⅓ cup nonfat dry milk powder
1 tablespoon dill seed
2 heaping tablespoons caraway seeds
2½ teaspoons salt
3 tablespoons canola or vegetable oil
2 to 2½ cups unbleached all-purpose flour

▸ Beat first 7 ingredients at medium speed with an electric mixer 1 minute or until blended. Add flour, ½ cup at a time, beating until dough pulls away from sides of bowl.
▸ Turn dough out onto a lightly floured surface and knead 3 minutes or until smooth and elastic, adding 1 tablespoon flour as needed to prevent sticking (dough will remain sticky).
▸ Place dough in a large greased bowl, turning to grease top. Cover with plastic wrap and let rise in a warm place (85°), free from drafts, 1½ to 2 hours or until doubled in bulk.
▸ Turn dough out onto a large baking sheet; shape into a loaf. Lightly sprinkle top with water. Cover and let rise in a warm place, free from drafts, 30 minutes or until doubled in bulk Lightly sprinkle top with water.
▸ Bake at 400° for 45 to 50 minutes or until loaf sounds hollow when tapped. Remove from pan and let cool on a wire rack.
Yield: 1 loaf

Boston Brown Bread

This steamed bread, traditionally served with baked beans, is also good toasted and spread with butter and honey.

1 cup whole wheat flour
1 cup rye flour
1 cup cornmeal
1 teaspoon salt
1 teaspoon baking soda
¾ cup dark molasses
2 cups buttermilk

▸ Grease two (1-pound) coffee cans.
▸ Combine all ingredients in a large bowl, stirring well.
▸ Pour batter into greased coffee cans and cover with a double thickness of aluminum foil. Tie securely with string.
▸ Place cans on a shallow rack in a large Dutch oven. Add water to a depth of one-third of the cans.
▸ Cover and bring water to a boil; steam 2 hours in boiling water, adding water as needed.
▸ Remove bread from cans and let cool on wire racks 10 minutes.
Yield: 2 loaves

Light-as-a-Feather Refrigerator Rolls

The perfect rolls to serve with carved meat for party sandwiches

1 cup shortening
1 cup sugar
1½ teaspoons salt
1 cup boiling water
2 large eggs
2 (¼-ounce) envelopes active dry yeast
1 cup warm water (105° to 115°)
6 cups flour (approximately)
¼ cup butter or margarine, melted

▸ Combine first 3 ingredients in a large bowl; add 1 cup boiling water and beat at medium speed with an electric mixer until shortening is melted and mixture has cooled slightly. Add eggs, beating to blend.

▸ Combine yeast and 1 cup warm water, stirring to dissolve; add to shortening mixture, beating well. Gradually add flour, ½ cup at a time, beating until a soft dough forms. If dough becomes too stiff for electric mixer, stir in remaining flour by hand.

▸ Cover and store in the refrigerator up to 10 days.

▸ Remove desired portion of dough and place on a lightly floured surface. Roll to less than ¼-inch thickness. Cut with a biscuit cutter and brush tops with melted butter; fold over lightly, pinching edges together.

▸ Place rolls on a lightly greased baking sheet. Cover and let rise in a warm place (85°), free from drafts, 1½ to 2 hours or until doubled in bulk.

▸ Bake at 425° for 10 to 15 minutes or until golden brown. Brush tops with melted butter.

Yield: 4 dozen

NOTE: To freeze: Shape rolls and place in aluminum foil pans. Cover and let rise to completely fill pans. Bake at 425° until set but not brown. Remove from oven and brush tops with melted butter. Let cool. Place pans in zip-top plastic bags and freeze. To serve, defrost and bake at 450° for 10 minutes or until golden brown.

Angel Biscuits

A combination from heaven - light as air but with the flavor of buttermilk biscuits

1 (¼-ounce) envelope active dry yeast
2 tablespoons warm water (105° to 115°)
5 cups all-purpose flour
1 teaspoon baking soda
1 tablespoon baking powder
1½ teaspoons salt
2 tablespoons sugar
1 cup shortening
2 cups buttermilk

▸ Combine yeast and 2 tablespoons warm water, stirring to dissolve.
▸ Sift together flour, baking soda, baking powder, salt, and sugar in a large bowl; Cut in shortening with a fork or pastry blender. Add buttermilk, stirring well. Add yeast mixture, stirring until dry ingredients are thoroughly moistened.
▸ Turn dough out onto a lightly floured surface and knead 1 to 2 minutes. Roll to desired thickness (½ inch) and cut into rounds. Brush tops with melted butter and place on an ungreased baking sheet.
▸ Bake at 400° for 12 to 15 minutes or until lightly browned. Freeze, if desired.

Yield: 2 to 3 dozen

NOTE: After mixing, dough may be refrigerated several days in a zip-top plastic bag or a covered bowl until ready to use. If using a plastic bag, leave a little room for dough to expand slightly. Biscuits may be rolled out and refrigerated overnight. Let stand at room temperature 1 hour before baking.

Overnight Spoon Rolls

Easy, light yeast rolls made from batter spooned into muffin pans.

1 (¼-ounce) envelope active dry yeast
2 cups warm water (105° to 115°)
4 cups self-rising flour
¼ cup sugar
¾ cup butter or margarine or shortening
1 large egg, lightly beaten

▸ Combine yeast and 2 cups warm water in a large bowl, stirring to dissolve. Add flour and remaining ingredients, stirring until blended. Cover and chill overnight.
▸ Grease muffin pans; spoon in batter, filling half full.
▸ Bake at 400° for 20 minutes or until golden brown.
Yield: 2 dozen

Popovers

These are like eating air wrapped in a thin layer of dough.

1 tablespoon butter
2 large eggs
1 cup milk
1 tablespoon butter, melted and cooled
1 cup all-purpose flour
¼ teaspoon salt

▸ Butter 8 muffin pan cups or 8 glass custard cups.
▸ Beat eggs at medium speed with an electric mixer until frothy; add milk, melted butter, flour, and salt, beating at low speed just until blended (batter will look like heavy cream - do not overbeat).
▸ Using a large spoon, fill buttered cups one-third full.
▸ Bake 20 minutes at 450°. Reduce oven temperature to 350° and bake 15 to 20 minutes or until popovers are brown and crisp and tops have puffed up.
▸ Turn muffin tin on its side and let popovers fall out. Loosen edges with a knife if they are stuck.
▸ Serve immediately with butter and jam.
Yield: 8 popovers

Lavosh - Processor Cracker Bread

Serve this Middle Eastern cracker bread with dips, spreads, and Tabbouleh (see page 73).

2⅓ cups all-purpose flour
½ teaspoon salt
½ teaspoon sugar
1 large egg
2 tablespoons butter or margarine
½ cup milk
3 tablespoons sesame seeds
1 tablespoon poppy seeds
Kosher salt to taste

▸ Process first 6 ingredients in a food processor until dough forms a ball. Cover and let stand at room temperature at least 1 hour.
▸ Flour 2 baking sheets and preheat oven to 475°.
▸ Turn dough out on a lightly floured surface and divide in half. Roll each portion to ⅛-inch thickness and brush off excess flour.
▸ Combine sesame and poppy seeds and sprinkle over dough. Lightly sprinkle with salt and transfer to floured baking sheets.
▸ Place 1 baking sheet on upper oven rack and place a pan of hot water on lower rack. Bake 5 minutes. Remove pan of water and reduce oven temperature to 350°. Bake 20 minutes or until bread is golden brown. Repeat procedure with second pan.
▸ Remove bread from baking sheet and let cool on a wire rack. Break bread into irregular pieces.
Yield: 2 lavosh

Rick's Tomato Crostini

A simply delicious bistro hit

1 baguette or 1 (16-ounce) unsliced French bread loaf
1 garlic clove, halved
2 medium tomatoes, seeded and chopped
3 tablespoons minced garlic
14 basil leaves, cut into thin strips
2 to 4 tablespoons balsamic vinegar
¼ cup olive oil
Salt and pepper to taste

▸ Cut bread into ¼ to ½-inch slices. Place on baking sheet.
▸ Bake at 400° for 5 minutes or until lightly browned. Rub hot bread with garlic, if desired.
▸ Combine tomatoes, minced garlic, basil, balsamic vinegar, and olive oil in a bowl. Stir thoroughly; add salt and pepper to taste. Let stand for 30 minutes.
▸ Serve with a slotted spoon alongside the toasted bread.
Yield: 3 dozen baguette slices or 2 dozen loaf slices

Lemon Crostini

An enticing and versatile canapé

1 (16-ounce) loaf French or Italian Bread
½ cup butter or margarine, softened
2 tablespoons chopped fresh parsley
3 garlic cloves, minced
1 teaspoon grated lemon rind

▸ Cut bread into 1-inch slices.
▸ Combine remaining ingredients in a bowl, stirring to blend.
▸ Spread over bread slices.
▸ Bake for 20 minutes at 300°.
Yield: 8 servings

Italian Biscuit Crostini

A perfect partner for the Tomato, Caper, Olive and Bleu Cheese Salad (see page 67)

1 (10 to 12-ounce) can refrigerated whole wheat biscuits
⅔ cup grated Parmesan cheese
½ cup mayonnaise
3 green onions, minced
½ teaspoon garlic powder
½ teaspoon dried Italian seasoning

▸ Separate biscuits and flatten each to a 5-inch circle on a lightly floured surface. Place on an ungreased baking sheet.
▸ Combine cheese and remaining ingredients and spread over biscuits to within ¼ inch of edges.
▸ Bake at 400° for 10 to 11 minutes or until golden brown. Cut biscuits into quarters and serve immediately.
Yield: 10 to 12 servings

Desserts

End of the Line

Coosa Valley Model Railroad

As a young boy watches a tiny train make its way across a river
bridge, his grandfather calls "Peter -- look here. See this building?"
They both peer through the glass at a streetscape of tiny structures.
"This is where the Center for Cultural Arts is now, but when your
grandmother and I were married, it was the Princess Theatre. We
couldn't afford a fancy honeymoon, so we celebrated by spending an
evening at the picture show. The movie was *My Friend Irma* with Dean
Martin. I'll never forget that night."

In 1988, when members of the Coosa Valley Model Railroad Club
began constructing a 72-foot model of Gadsden with working
railroads, they believed many people would enjoy seeing the exhibit.
Today, thousands of the Center's visitors gather at the model each
year to reminisce about what life was like in the 1940's.

Using more than 700 feet of track, 3 miles of wiring and 1,400 wooden
screws, the club's members laid the groundwork for the miniature
railroad system that would support six trains simultaneously. Working
from old photographs and their own memories, they fashioned
Gadsden's historic buildings using materials like photo negatives for
windows and scrap foam board for walls.

Completion of the Gadsden model was a landmark event at the Center.
In olden days when a railroad company celebrated the completion of a
line, they marked the occasion by driving a golden spike into the
track. When Center visitors look closely near the Emma Sansom
statue just before the track crosses the Coosa River, they can see the
tiny golden nail, made by a local jeweler, that serves as the model
railroad's final spike.

Easy Triple Chocolate Torte

It's easy and low fat; try it, you'll love it and make it often.

¼ cup unsweetened cocoa
3 tablespoons all-purpose flour
¼ teaspoon baking powder
1 cup granulated sugar, divided
4 (1-ounce) bittersweet chocolate squares, finely chopped (we prefer
  Ghirardelli)
½ cup boiling water
2 egg yolks
2 tablespoons chocolate liqueur
4 egg whites
Sifted powdered sugar

▸ Lightly grease an 8-inch springform pan.
▸ Combine first 3 ingredients and ½ cup granulated sugar in a large bowl; add
  chocolate and ½ cup boiling water, stirring until chocolate melts. Stir in egg
  yolks and liqueur.
▸ Beat egg whites at high speed with an electric mixer until foamy; add ½
  cup granulated sugar, 1 tablespoon at a time, beating 2 to 4 minutes or just
  until moist, stiff peaks form.
▸ Fold one-third of egg whites into chocolate mixture; fold in remaining egg
  whites just until there are no streaks of egg white. Pour batter into greased
  springform pan.
▸ Bake at 375° for 28 minutes or until a wooden pick inserted in center
  comes out clean. Remove from oven and let cool on a wire rack 10 minutes.
  Remove sides from pan and let cool completely on wire rack. (Cake top will
  be cracked.)
▸ Lightly dust cake with powdered sugar and serve.
Yield: 10 servings

Amaretto Flan

An impressive baked custard with caramel sauce that you can have ready for the oven in less than 30 minutes.

½ cup sugar
1 (14-ounce) can sweetened condensed milk
1 cup half-and-half
½ cup amaretto or almond-flavored liqueur
3 large eggs
3 egg yolks
Sliced peaches, apricots, or strawberries

▸ Sprinkle sugar in a 9-inch round cakepan; place over medium heat. Hold pan using oven mitts and caramelize sugar by shaking pan occasionally until sugar melts and turns a golden brown color; let cool. (Mixture may crack slightly as it cools.)
▸ Combine condensed milk, half-and-half, liqueur, eggs, and egg yolks in container of an electric blender; process at high speed for about 15 seconds. Pour mixture over caramelized sugar.
▸ Cover cakepan with aluminum foil and place in a larger shallow pan. Pour hot water to a depth of 1 inch in larger pan.
▸ Bake at 350° for 55 minutes or until a knife inserted in center comes out clean. Remove pan from water and uncover; let cool on a wire rack at least 30 minutes. Loosen edges with a spatula.
▸ Invert flan onto a serving plate and arrange fruit around edges.
Yield: 1 (9-inch) flan

Decadent Chocolate-Almond Torte

Using premium chocolate will make this extra special.

1 cup (5 ounces) whole almonds, toasted and cooled
2 tablespoons granulated sugar
2 tablespoons vegetable oil
¾ cup unsalted butter
½ cup whipping cream
2 (8-ounce) packages bittersweet chocolate squares, finely chopped
6 large eggs, separated
⅓ cup granulated sugar
1 cup whipping cream, chilled
2 tablespoons amaretto or almond-flavored liqueur or
   1 teaspoon almond extract
2 tablespoons granulated sugar
Powdered sugar
½ cup sliced almonds, toasted

▸ Position rack in center of oven. Butter and flour a 9 x 3-inch springform pan; shake out excess flour. Line bottom of pan with parchment or wax paper. Butter paper.
▸ Pulse ½ cup whole almonds and 2 tablespoons granulated sugar in a food processor until finely ground. Transfer mixture to a large bowl. Process remaining ½ cup almonds and oil in food processor until mixture is thick and pasty (similar to peanut butter), scraping down sides frequently.
▸ Cook butter and ½ cup whipping cream in a large heavy saucepan over medium heat until butter is melted and mixture is simmering. Remove from heat and whisk in chocolate until smooth. Stir in both almond mixtures and let cool slightly.
▸ Beat egg whites at medium speed with an electric mixer until soft peaks form; gradually add ⅓ cup granulated sugar, beating until stiff peaks form.
▸ Beat egg yolks in a separate large bowl at medium speed 5 minutes or until thick and pale. Gradually add chocolate mixture to egg yolks, beating until blended. Fold in egg whites, one-third at a time. Pour batter into prepared pan.
▸ Bake at 350° for 35 minutes or until sides crack and puff and a wooden pick inserted in center comes out with moist batter attached. Remove from oven and let cool on a wire rack 2 hours or until room temperature.
▸ Beat chilled whipping cream, liqueur, and 2 tablespoons granulated sugar at high speed until soft peaks form.
▸ Run a small sharp knife around sides of pan to loosen cake. Remove sides of pan. Dust cake with powdered sugar and sprinkle with toasted almond slices. Serve chilled or at room temperature with whipped cream.
Yield: 1 (9-inch) torte

Daugette's Charlotte Russe

A favorite Southern dessert updated with a cooked egg custard

16 to 20 unfilled ladyfingers, split
2 envelopes unflavored gelatin
½ cup water
6 large eggs, separated
1 cup sugar, divided
¼ teaspoon salt
¼ cup bourbon, rum, or sherry
2 cups whipping cream, whipped

▸ Line bottom and sides of an 8 or 9 x 3-inch springform pan with ladyfingers.
▸ Sprinkle gelatin over ½ cup water; let stand 5 minutes.
▸ Beat egg yolks, ½ cup sugar, and salt with a handheld mixer in the top of a double boiler. Gradually beat in gelatin mixture. Cook over boiling water, stirring constantly, 10 minutes or until mixture starts to thicken.
▸ Pour mixture into a large bowl and chill, stirring occasionally, 30 minutes or until mixture begins to thicken. Stir in bourbon.
▸ Combine egg whites and remaining ½ cup sugar in top of double boiler. Cook over low heat, beating with handheld mixer until soft peaks form. Remove from heat and let cool slightly.
▸ Fold egg whites and whipped cream into gelatin mixture. Spoon into ladyfinger-lined pan. Chill 3 hours or overnight.
▸ Carefully remove sides of pan and serve.
Yield: 12 servings

Fresh Pineapple Compote

For a party presentation, serve in crystal sherbet/champagne glasses.

1 large ripe pineapple
¼ cup powdered sugar
½ cup cherry brandy
2 (16-ounce) cans pitted dark, sweet cherries, chilled

▸ Remove leafy top of pineapple. Slice pineapple lengthwise and cut each half into 4 wedges. Cut fruit from each wedge, into ½-inch cubes.
▸ Place pineapple chunks in a large glass bowl, sprinkle with powdered sugar and toss well; add brandy and toss gently. Cover with plastic wrap and chill 8 hours or overnight, tossing once or twice.
▸ Drain juice from cherries just before serving; add cherries to pineapple mixture.
▸ Serve with cookies or pound cake, if desired.
Yield: 8 servings

Tiramisu

An Italian trifle with layers of creamy cheese custard, grated chocolate, and ladyfingers brushed with coffee and liqueur

6 egg yolks
1½ cups sugar, divided
1 cup mascarpone cheese
1 cup whipping cream, whipped
⅓ cup water
2 tablespoons espresso or double-strength brewed coffee
½ cup sweet Marsala wine
2 (3-ounce) packages ladyfingers
1 (8-ounce) chocolate bar, shaved with a vegetable peeler

▸ Combine egg yolks and 1¼ cups sugar in top of double boiler; beat at medium speed with a handheld mixer in the top of a double boiler until thick and lemon colored. Bring water to a boil; reduce heat to low and cook egg yolk mixture, stirring constantly, 8 to 10 minutes. Remove from heat.
▸ Add mascarpone cheese to egg yolk mixture, beating until smooth. Fold in whipped cream.
▸ Bring ⅓ cup water and remaining ¼ cup sugar to a boil in a small saucepan; reduce heat and simmer until sugar is dissolved. Remove from heat and let cool. Stir in espresso and Marsala. Brush mixture on cut sides of ladyfingers.
▸ Line sides of an 8-inch springform pan or a 3-quart soufflé dish with ladyfingers; pour half of filling in and sprinkle with half of chocolate shavings. Repeat layers once.

Yield: 10 to 12 servings

NOTE: *As a substitute for mascarpone cheese, beat 1 (8-ounce) package cream cheese, 3 tablespoons sour cream, and 2 tablespoons whipping cream at medium speed with an electric mixer until creamy.*

French Chocolate Roulage

Impress your guests.

Cake
6 large eggs, separated
¾ cup granulated sugar, divided
⅓ cup unsweetened cocoa
1½ teaspoons vanilla extract
Pinch of salt
2 to 3 tablespoons powdered sugar or unsweetened cocoa, sifted
Sifted powdered sugar

- ► Grease bottom and sides of a 15 x 10-inch jelly-roll pan; line with wax paper. Grease and flour wax paper.
- ► Beat egg whites at high speed with an electric mixer until moist, stiff peaks form.
- ► Beat egg yolks in a separate bowl at high speed 4 to 5 minutes or until foamy; gradually add ½ cup granulated sugar and beat 5 minutes or until thick and pale. Gradually add cocoa, vanilla, and salt, beating at low speed just until blended.
- ► Fold egg whites into yolk mixture, one-third at a time. Pour batter into prepared pan, gently spreading evenly.
- ► Bake at 375° for 15 minutes or until a wooden pick inserted in center comes out clean.
- ► Sift 2 tablespoons powdered sugar over cake. Place a clean dish towel over cake; place a baking sheet, right side down, over cloth. Grip ends of jelly-roll pan and baking sheet and invert cake. Place on counter. Gently lift jelly-roll pan off of cake. Carefully remove wax paper.
- ► Roll cake and towel, jelly-roll fashion, starting at a short side. Place, seam side down, on a wire rack and let cool.

Whipped Cream Filling
2 cups whipping cream
⅓ cup powdered sugar
1 teaspoon vanilla extract
1 cup pecans or walnuts, toasted and chopped

- ► Beat whipping cream in a chilled bowl with chilled beaters at high speed with an electric mixer until soft peaks form.
- ► Gradually add powdered sugar and vanilla, beating until stiff peaks form. Fold in nuts.

OR

Ice Cream Filling
½ gallon vanilla ice cream, softened
1 cup pecans or walnuts, toasted and chopped

▸ Combine ice cream and nuts, stirring well.
▸ Unroll cake, remove towel, and spread Whipped Cream Filling or Ice-Cream Filling evenly over top, leaving a 1-inch border around edges. Re-roll cake and place, seam side down, on a baking sheet. Cover and chill whipped cream roll or freeze ice-cream roll until ready to serve.
▸ Sprinkle cake roll with powdered sugar and slice to serve.
Yield: 10 servings

Rum Trifle

Light rum can also be used to spark this crowd pleaser.

½ cup dark rum
¾ cup slivered almonds, toasted
¾ cup golden raisins
1 (3.4-ounce) package vanilla pudding mix
2½ cups milk
1 cup whipping cream, whipped and divided
1 (10-ounce) angel food cake, cut into ½-inch cubes
Slivered almonds, toasted
Whole strawberries

▸ Combine first 3 ingredients in a bowl; let stand 1 hour.
▸ Prepare pudding according to package directions using 2½ cups milk. Chill until set. Fold in half of whipped cream.
▸ Place one-third of angel food cake cubes in a trifle bowl or a large serving bowl, covering the bottom. Top with one-third of raisin mixture and one-third of pudding. Repeat layers twice.
▸ Spread remaining whipped cream over top. Sprinkle with slivered almonds and garnish with whole strawberries. Chill.
Yield: 8 to 10 servings

Bread Pudding

A world famous blues musician once recommended using day-old biscuits instead of French bread.

Pudding
1 (16-ounce) day-old French bread loaf, cut into 1½ to 2-inch cubes
   (about 12 cups)
2 apples, peeled and thinly sliced
½ cup raisins (optional)
1 cup chopped toasted pecans (optional)
4 cups milk
1 cup sugar
½ cup butter
3 large eggs
1 teaspoon ground cinnamon
¼ teaspoon ground nutmeg
½ teaspoon vanilla extract
½ teaspoon salt

▶ Grease a 13 x 9 x 2-inch baking dish. Place bread cubes in bottom of dish. Top with apple slices and, if desired, raisins and pecans.
▶ Scald milk in a heavy saucepan over medium heat; add sugar and butter, stirring until melted. Remove from heat and let cool 10 minutes.
▶ Beat eggs at medium speed with an electric mixer; gradually add cooled milk mixture, spices, vanilla, and salt, beating well. Pour over apple slices.
▶ Bake at 325° for 45 to 50 minutes or until a knife inserted in center comes out clean.

Brandy Sauce
¼ cup butter
½ cup milk
¼ cup sugar
3 large eggs
¼ cup brandy, bourbon, or dark rum
⅛ teaspoon ground cloves

▶ Melt butter in a medium saucepan over medium heat; stir in milk and sugar.
▶ Beat eggs with a wire whisk in a small bowl; gradually stir in a small amount of hot milk mixture. Add egg mixture to remaining hot milk mixture and cook over low heat, stirring constantly, 3 to 4 minutes or until thickened. Stir in brandy.
▶ Serve sauce on the side, warm or chilled.
Yield: about 1½ cups

Ambrosia Roulage

A fruit-filled delight

¼ cup butter
1 (8-ounce) can crushed pineapple, well drained
1 cup flaked coconut
1 cup fresh orange sections, chopped and drained
1 (14-ounce) can sweetened condensed milk
1 cup all-purpose flour
¼ teaspoon baking soda
¼ teaspoon salt
¼ teaspoon ground ginger
3 large eggs
1 cup granulated sugar
⅓ cup fresh orange juice
1 teaspoon vanilla extract
Powdered sugar
Whipped cream

- Line a 15 x 10-inch jelly-roll pan with aluminum foil; put butter in pan and place in oven until melted. Spread butter evenly on foil.
- Combine pineapple, coconut, and chopped orange in a bowl, stirring well. Spoon mixture evenly into pan. Drizzle with condensed milk; set aside.
- Combine flour, baking soda, salt, and ginger in a small bowl.
- Beat eggs at medium speed with an electric mixer 2 minutes or until light and fluffy; gradually add granulated sugar, beating well. Add flour mixture, orange juice, and vanilla, beating until smooth. Pour over fruit in pan.
- Bake at 375° for 20 to 25 minutes or until cake springs back lightly when touched or a wooden pick inserted in center comes out clean. Remove from oven and sprinkle generously with powdered sugar.
- Place a clean dish towel over cake; and place a baking sheet, right side down, over cloth. Grip ends of jelly-roll pan and baking sheet and invert cake. Place on counter. Gently lift jelly-roll pan off of cake. Carefully remove foil.
- Roll cake up, jelly-roll fashion, starting at a short side. Wrap towel around roll and let stand 10 minutes or just until cool. (Do not leave in towel too long or cake will become dry.)
- Remove towel from around roll and sprinkle roll with powdered sugar. Cut into 1-inch thick slices and serve with whipped cream.

NOTE: If you do not plan to serve the cake shortly after it has cooled, remove the towel and cover the cake with plastic wrap.
Yield: 10 servings

Pralines

"When we grandkids visited in the summer, my grandmother would make Pralines, if the weather was right."

2 cups granulated sugar
1 cup firmly packed brown sugar
½ cup light corn syrup
1 (6-ounce) can evaporated milk
½ cup butter
1 teaspoon vanilla extract
2 to 3 cups pecan halves

▸ Cook first 4 ingredients in a heavy 3-quart saucepan over low heat, stirring gently, until sugar dissolves. Cover and cook over medium heat 2 to 3 minutes to wash down sugar crystals from sides of pan. Uncover and cook, stirring constantly, until a candy thermometer registers 235° (soft ball stage). Remove candy syrup from heat.
▸ Add butter and vanilla and beat with a wooden spoon until creamy; stir in nuts.
▸ Working rapidly, drop mixture by tablespoonfuls onto greased wax paper.
Yield: about 2½ dozen
NOTE: *For best results, avoid making this when the humidity is high.*

Raspberry Sauce

Great to serve over fruit, ice cream, and cheesecake

1 (10-ounce) package frozen raspberries, thawed
3 tablespoons apricot preserves
2 tablespoons orange flavored liqueur (we prefer Grand Marnier)
1 tablespoon lemon juice

▸ Process all ingredients in a blender until blended well. Pour through a wire-mesh strainer, discarding seeds. Chill.
▸ Serve over fruits, pound cakes, cheesecakes, ice cream, or chocolate roulage.
Yield: 1½ cups

Mocha Party Cakes

This angel food cake with coffee-flavored icing, rolled in crunchy peanuts is a favorite from The Blue Moon Inn in Montgomery.

Cake
1 (16-ounce) package angel food cake mix

- Prepare cake mix according to package directions; spread batter in an ungreased 15 x 10-inch jelly-roll pan.
- Bake at 325° for 1 hour or until cake pulls away from sides of pan. Remove from oven and let cool completely on a wire rack.
- Remove cake from pan and remove soft brown crust from cake. Slice cake 5 times lengthwise and 10 times crosswise using a serrated knife.

Mocha Icing
1 tablespoon instant coffee granules
1 tablespoon hot water
1 cup butter, softened
1 (16-ounce) package powdered sugar
2 (12-ounce) cans salted skinless cocktail peanuts, toasted and coarsely chopped

- Combine coffee granules and 1 tablespoon hot water, stirring until coffee is dissolved.
- Beat butter at medium speed with an electric mixer until light and fluffy. Add half of sugar, beating well. Add half of coffee mixture, beating well. Add remaining half of sugar and coffee mixture in small amounts, beating well until icing is very fluffy. Add additional hot water if needed.
- Spread Mocha Icing generously on 5 sides of cake squares and roll in chopped nuts.

Yield: 50 cakes

Calypso Ice Cream Pie

Sinfully delicious

Chocolate Sauce
3 (1-ounce) squares unsweetened chocolate
¼ cup butter
⅔ cup granulated sugar
⅛ teaspoon salt
⅔ cup evaporated milk
1 teaspoon vanilla extract
⅛ teaspoon almond extract

▸ Cook chocolate and butter in a heavy saucepan over low heat, stirring
   often, until chocolate melts.
▸ Remove from heat and gradually stir in granulated sugar and salt until
   blended. Add evaporated milk, stirring well.
▸ Return mixture to low heat and cook, stirring constantly, 4 minutes.
▸ Remove from heat and stir in extracts. Chill thoroughly.

Pie
2 cups crushed cream-filled chocolate sandwich cookies crushed
   (about 22 cookies)
½ cup butter or margarine, melted
½ cup granulated sugar
2 pints coffee ice cream, slightly softened
1 cup whipping cream
3 tablespoons powdered sugar
1 cup chopped pecans

▸ Combine cookie crumbs, butter, and granulated sugar, stirring well. Press
   on bottom and up sides of a 10-inch pie plate. Freeze 1 hour or until firm.
▸ Remove cookie crust from freezer. Spread ice cream smoothly over crust.
   Freeze 1 hour or until firm.
▸ Remove Chocolate Sauce from the refrigerator and let stand at room
   temperature about 1 hour.
▸ Spread sauce evenly over ice cream and freeze 1 hour or until firm.
▸ Beat whipping cream at high speed with an electric mixer until soft peaks
   form. Add powdered sugar, beating until stiff peaks form. Spread over
   Chocolate Sauce and sprinkle with pecans.
▸ Freeze pie 4 hours or until firm. For easy serving, dip bottom of pie plate in
   hot water a few seconds. Slice and serve.
Yield: 8 to 10 servings

Chocolate-Nut Ice Cream Torte

A chocoholic's delight

½ gallon chocolate ice cream, softened
1 cup crushed chocolate wafers
1 cup miniature marshmallows
½ cup coarsely chopped pecans
½ cup whipping cream, whipped

▸ Combine first 4 ingredients in a bowl, stirring until blended. Spoon mixture into a 10-cup mold or springform pan and freeze 3 hours or until firm.

Smooth Chocolate Sauce
1 cup (6 ounces) semi-sweet chocolate morsels
½ cup whipping cream
½ teaspoon vanilla extract

▸ Cook chocolate and whipping cream in a saucepan over low heat, stirring constantly, until chocolate is melted. Remove from heat and stir in vanilla. Let cool.
▸ Unmold torte and place on a serving platter. Pipe whipped cream around the base and serve with Smooth Chocolate Sauce.
Yield: 10 servings

Frozen Yogurt Fruit Pops

Cool treats with "good-for-you stuff"

5 large strawberries, chopped
1 banana
1 cup plain yogurt
½ cup applesauce
¼ cup apple juice
1 tablespoon honey
Wooden ice-cream sticks

▸ Combine chopped strawberries, banana, yogurt, applesauce, apple juice, and honey in a large bowl, stirring to blend well.
▸ Spoon mixture into 5 (5-ounce) paper cups, dividing evenly among cups.
▸ Cover each cup with aluminum foil. Make a hole in the center of each piece of foil and insert a wooden ice-cream stick through the hole into the center of the mixture to the bottom of the cup.
▸ Place cups in freezer and freeze 4 hours or until completely frozen.
▸ Remove foil and peel off paper cup to serve.
Yield: 5 pops

Orange Cream Dream

A sweet way to slip in another fruit for the day

2 tablespoons frozen orange juice concentrate, thawed and undiluted
1 banana, sliced
2 scoops low-fat vanilla ice cream or frozen yogurt
¼ teaspoon vanilla extract
3 ice cubes

> ‣ Combine first 4 ingredients in a blender; place cover on top and process at medium speed 30 seconds or until smooth.
> ‣ Add ice cubes and pulse 3 or 4 times; process at high speed 45 seconds or until smooth.
> ‣ Pour into a tall glass and serve with a straw.

Yield: 1 serving

Team Cream

Kids (and adults) love the can-inside-a-can method of making ice cream and sherbet. Choose partners and sit about 3 feet apart. Put on mitts or gloves and start rolling.

1 cup milk
1 cup whipping cream
½ cup sugar
½ teaspoon vanilla extract
Nuts, fruit, or sauces as desired
1 (16-ounce) coffee can with plastic lid
1 (#10) can with plastic lid (restaurant/commercial cans)
1 bag crushed ice
¾ cup rock salt

> ‣ Combine first 5 ingredients in clean coffee can, stirring with a spoon until well blended. Put plastic lid on securely.
> ‣ Place coffee can in #10 can and fill around and above with crushed ice and rock salt. Put plastic lid on securely.
> ‣ Roll can-in-a-can between 4 team members sitting on cushions and wearing oven mitts until ice cream is frozen.

Southern Pecan Pie

What's a cookbook without a great pecan pie recipe?

3 large eggs
1¼ cups sugar
1 cup light corn syrup
¼ cup butter, melted
¼ teaspoon vanilla extract
Pinch of salt
1 cup pecan halves
1 unbaked 9-inch pastry shell

▸ Beat eggs in a medium bowl with a fork or a wire whisk until blended; add sugar, corn syrup, butter, vanilla, and salt, stirring well. Stir in pecans.
▸ Pour mixture into pastry shell.
▸ Bake at 400° for 15 minutes. Reduce oven temperature to 350° and bake 25 to 30 minutes or until a sharp knife inserted near center comes out with little bits of filling attached. (Edges should be set but center should quiver slightly.)
Yield: 6 to 8 servings

Lemon Angel Pie

A little slice of heaven

4 large eggs, separated
1½ cups granulated sugar, divided
½ teaspoon cream of tartar
Grated rind and juice of 1½ lemons
1 cup whipping cream
2 tablespoons sifted powdered sugar
Garnish: lemon slices

▸ Lightly grease a 10-inch pie plate.
▸ Beat egg whites at high speed with an electric mixer until foamy; gradually add 1 cup granulated sugar and cream of tartar, beating until stiff peaks form. Spoon into greased pie plate shaping a crust.
▸ Bake at 250° for 30 minutes. Turn oven off; crack oven door and let crust cool in oven 8 hours or overnight.
▸ Combine egg yolks, lemon rind, lemon juice, and remaining ½ cup granulated sugar in the top of a double boiler; cook over boiling water, stirring constantly, until thickened. Pour over meringue crust and let cool completely.
▸ Beat whipping cream at high speed with an electric mixer until foamy; add powdered sugar and beat until stiff peaks form. Spread over filling. Garnish, if desired.
Yield: 1 (10-inch) pie

Blueberry Tart

An easy filling mixed in a blender and baked in the crust.

Tart Crust
1⅓ cups all-purpose flour
¼ teaspoon salt
2 tablespoons sugar
½ cup unsalted butter, chilled and cut into pieces
1 egg yolk
1 to 2 tablespoons ice water

▸ Pulse first 3 ingredients in a food processor to blend; add butter and pulse 5 seconds or until mixture is crumbly.
▸ Add egg yolk and 1 tablespoon water and process, stopping to scrape down sides. Add remaining 1 tablespoon water, a few drops at a time, through the food chute, processing until dough forms a ball. Wrap dough in plastic wrap and shape into a disc. Chill 1 hour.
▸ Roll dough into a circle on a lightly floured surface; transfer to an 11-inch tart pan with a removable bottom. Trim edges. Cover with aluminum foil and place rice or pie weights on foil.
▸ Bake at 425° for 8 to 10 minutes. Remove weights and foil and bake 5 to 10 more minutes or until crust is dry but not browned. Remove from oven and let cool completely on a wire rack. (Crust can be prepared a day ahead.)

Filling
2 tablespoons all-purpose flour
2 cups fresh blueberries
1 cup buttermilk
3 egg yolks
½ cup granulated sugar
1 tablespoon lemon rind
1 tablespoon fresh lemon juice
¼ cup butter, melted and cooled
1 teaspoon vanilla extract
½ teaspoon salt
Powdered sugar

▸ Combine flour and blueberries in a zip-top plastic bag; seal and shake to coat well. Pour into Tart Crust.
▸ Combine buttermilk, egg yolks, granulated sugar, lemon rind, lemon juice, butter, vanilla, and salt in a blender and mix on high until thoroughly blended. Pour over blueberries.
▸ Bake at 350° for 30 to 35 minutes or until set. Remove from oven and let cool completely on a wire rack.
▸ Remove sides of pan; dust with powdered sugar and serve.
Yield: 1 (11-inch) tart

Blueberry Pie

The soft cheesecake texture and streusel topping make this pie scrumptious.

Pie
1 (8-ounce) package cream cheese, softened
1 (8-ounce) container sour cream
¾ cup sugar
1 tablespoon vanilla extract
2 cups fresh blueberries
¼ cup all-purpose flour
1 unbaked 9-inch deep-dish pastry shell

‣ Beat first 4 ingredients at high speed with an electric mixer until creamy.
‣ Combine blueberries and flour in a zip-top plastic bag; seal and shake to coat well. Discard extra flour.
‣ Fold blueberries into cream cheese mixture. Pour into pastry shell.
‣ Bake at 350° for 40 to 45 minutes or until set in the center.

Streusel Topping
¼ cup all-purpose flour
⅓ cup sugar
¼ cup butter, melted
1 cup pecans, finely chopped

‣ Combine all ingredients, stirring until blended.
‣ Spoon Streusel Topping over pie and bake 15 more minutes.
Yield: 1 (9-inch) pie

Coconut Pie

"This is my mother's recipe, which makes it special and also very good."

¾ cup margarine, softened
2 cups sugar
4 large eggs
1½ teaspoons distilled vinegar
1½ teaspoons vanilla extract
1 (12-ounce) package frozen flaked coconut, thawed
2 unbaked 9-inch pastry shells

‣ Beat margarine and sugar at high speed with an electric mixer until creamy; add eggs, beating until blended. Stir in vinegar, vanilla, and coconut.
‣ Divide mixture evenly between 2 pastry shells.
‣ Bake at 325° for 1 hour or until set in the center.
Yield: 2 (9-inch) pies

Chocolate Fudge Pie

Chocolatey and heavenly - calorie watchers beware!

2 large eggs, separated
2 tablespoons sugar
1 (14-ounce) can sweetened condensed milk
¼ teaspoon salt
1 cup (6 ounces) semi-sweet chocolate morsels
1 teaspoon vanilla extract
2 tablespoons all-purpose flour
½ cup coarsely chopped nuts
1 unbaked 9-inch pastry shell

▸ Beat egg whites at high speed with an electric mixer until soft peaks form. Gradually add sugar, beating until stiff peaks form. Set aside.
▸ Bring condensed milk and salt to a boil in a saucepan over medium heat, stirring constantly. Remove from heat.
▸ Add chocolate, vanilla, and flour to milk mixture, beating well with a wooden spoon. Add egg yolks, one at a time, beating well after each addition. Stir in nuts and fold in egg whites. Pour mixture into pastry shell.
▸ Bake at 350° for 40 minutes or until firm.
Yield: 1 (9-inch) pie

Irish Cream Chocolate Chip Cheesecake

It's the liqueur that makes it special.

Graham Cracker Crust
2 cups graham cracker crumbs
¼ cup sugar
6 tablespoons butter, melted
½ cup (3 ounces) semi-sweet chocolate morsels

▸ Coat a 9-inch springform pan with vegetable cooking spray.
▸ Combine cracker crumbs and sugar in a bowl; stir in butter. Press mixture in the bottom and 1 inch up the sides of greased pan.
▸ Bake at 325° for 7 minutes or until lightly browned. Remove from oven. Sprinkle chocolate morsels over warm crust.

Filling
4½ (8-ounce) packages cream cheese, softened
1⅔ cups sugar
5 large eggs
1 cup Irish cream liqueur
1 tablespoon vanilla extract
½ cup (3 ounces) semi-sweet chocolate morsels

▸ Beat cream cheese at high speed with an electric mixer until creamy; gradually add sugar, beating well. Add eggs, one at a time, beating just until yellow disappears after each addition. Stir in liqueur and vanilla.
▸ Top with cream cheese mixture. Sprinkle with chocolate morsels.
▸ Bake at 325° for 1 hour and 20 minutes or almost set and a wooden pick inserted in center comes out almost clean.

Coffee Cream
1 cup whipping cream, chilled
2 tablespoons sugar
1 teaspoon instant coffee granules

▸ Beat all ingredients at high speed with an electric mixer until stiff peaks form.
▸ Spread Coffee Cream over cooled cake.
Yield: 8 servings

Iris' Cheesecake Supreme

A smooth and creamy cheesecake with a lemon-flavored cookie-like crust

Crust
1 cup all-purpose flour
¼ cup sugar
1 teaspoon grated lemon rind
½ cup butter or margarine, cut into pieces
1 egg yolk, lightly beaten
¼ teaspoon vanilla extract

▶ Combine first 3 ingredients in a bowl; cut in butter with a fork or pastry blender until mixture is crumbly. Add egg yolk and vanilla, stirring until well blended.

▶ Press one-third of dough on the bottom of a 9-inch springform pan with sides removed.

▶ Bake at 400° for 8 minutes or until golden. Remove from oven and let cool on a wire rack.

▶ Attach sides of pan; grease sides and press remaining dough to a height of 1¾ inches around sides.

Filling
5 (8-ounce) packages cream cheese, softened
¼ teaspoon vanilla extract
¾ teaspoon grated lemon rind
1¾ cups sugar
3 tablespoons all-purpose flour
¼ teaspoon salt
4 or 5 large eggs (1 cup total)
2 egg yolks
¼ cup whipping cream

▶ Beat cream cheese at high speed with an electric mixer until creamy; add vanilla and lemon rind, beating well.

▶ Combine sugar, flour, and salt in a bowl; gradually add to cream cheese mixture, beating until blended. Add eggs and egg yolks, one at a time, beating just until yellow disappears after each addition. Gently stir in whipping cream.

▶ Pour batter into crust.

▶ Bake at 450° for 12 minutes. Reduce oven temperature to 300° and bake 55 minutes or until center is almost set and a knife blade inserted in center comes out almost clean. Remove from oven and let cool on a wire rack 30 minutes.

▶ Loosen sides of cheesecake using a spatula. Let cool 30 minutes. Remove sides of pan and let cool 2 hours.

Strawberry Glaze
2 to 3 cups fresh strawberries, divided
1 cup water
1½ tablespoons cornstarch
½ to ¾ cup sugar (depending on sweetness of berries)

▸ Crush 1 cup strawberries in a saucepan; add 1 cup water and cook over medium heat 2 minutes. Pour mixture through a wire-mesh strainer, pressing berries through. Discard seeds.
▸ Combine cornstarch and sugar; gradually stir into hot strawberry mixture. Bring to a boil over medium heat and cook one minute, stirring gently. Remove from heat and let cool to room temperature.
▸ Place remaining whole strawberries on cooled cheesecake. Pour glaze over strawberries.
▸ Top cheesecake with Strawberry Glaze and chill 2 hours.
Yield: 1 (9-inch) cheesecake

Blueberry Cheesecake

A luscious lower-fat cheesecake with a layer of blueberries in the filling and on top

1 cup all-purpose flour
½ cup margarine, softened
1 tablespoon vinegar
1 (8-ounce) package Neufchâtel low-fat cream cheese, softened
1 cup skim milk
⅔ cup sugar, divided
1 large egg
4 cups blueberries, divided
2 tablespoons cornstarch
⅛ teaspoon grated lemon rind
⅛ teaspoon ground nutmeg

▸ Coat an 8-inch springform pan with vegetable cooking spray.
▸ Process first 3 ingredients in a food processor until mixture is crumbly. Press in the bottom and 1-inch up the sides of pan.
▸ Bake at 400° for 5 to 8 minutes or just until lightly browned.
▸ Process cream cheese, milk, ⅓ cup sugar, and egg in food processor until smooth. Pour over prepared crust.
▸ Cook 3 cups of blueberries and cornstarch in a saucepan over medium heat, stirring constantly, until thickened. Pour over cream cheese mixture.
▸ Bake at 350° for 45 minutes or until set. Remove from oven and let cool on a wire rack.
▸ Combine remaining 1 cup blueberries, remaining ⅓ cup sugar, lemon rind, and nutmeg, tossing to coat. Arrange over cooled cheesecake.
Yield: 1 (8-inch) cheesecake

Old-Fashioned Chocolate Sheet Cake

When iced, this cake will stay moist for days.

Cake
2 cups all-purpose flour
2 cups granulated sugar
½ cup butter
3 tablespoons unsweetened cocoa
½ cup vegetable oil
1 cup water
2 large eggs
½ cup buttermilk
1 teaspoon baking soda
½ teaspoon salt
1 teaspoon vanilla extract

▸ Grease a 13 x 9 x 2-inch pan.
▸ Combine flour and sugar in a large bowl.
▸ Bring butter, cocoa, oil, and 1 cup water to a boil in a heavy saucepan over medium heat, stirring constantly. Gradually whisk into flour mixture.
▸ Add eggs, buttermilk, baking soda, salt, and vanilla to flour mixture, whisking well. Pour batter into greased pan.
▸ Bake at 350° for 40 minutes or until a wooden pick inserted in center comes out clean.

Chocolate Icing
½ cup butter
3 tablespoons unsweetened cocoa
6 tablespoons buttermilk
1(16-ounce) package powdered sugar
1 tablespoon vanilla extract
1 cup chopped nuts

▸ Bring first 3 ingredients to a boil, stirring constantly, in a heavy saucepan. Remove from heat.
▸ Add powdered sugar and vanilla, stirring until smooth. Stir in nuts.
▸ Spread warm Chocolate Icing over top of cake.
Yield: 12 to 15 servings

Oatmeal Cake

"So-o-o-o yummy. What a treat!"

Cake
1 cup uncooked quick-cooking oats
1 cup boiling water
½ cup butter, softened
1 cup granulated sugar
1 cup firmly packed brown sugar
2 large eggs
1 teaspoon vanilla extract
1 cup all-purpose flour
1 teaspoon baking soda
½ teaspoon salt
1 teaspoon ground cinnamon
½ teaspoon ground nutmeg
1¾ cups chopped dates
1 cup chopped pecans

▸ Grease and flour a 13 x 9 x 2-inch pan.
▸ Combine oats and 1 cup boiling water, stirring well. Let stand 20 minutes.
▸ Beat butter and sugars at high speed with an electric mixer until creamy; add eggs, one at a time, beating well after each addition. Add oatmeal and vanilla, beating well.
▸ Combine flour, baking soda, salt, cinnamon, and nutmeg; add to oatmeal mixture, stirring just until dry ingredients are moistened. Fold in dates and pecans. Pour batter into prepared pan.
▸ Bake at 350° for 35 to 40 minutes or until a wooden pick inserted in center comes out clean. Remove from oven and let cool slightly on a wire rack.

Coconut Topping
6 tablespoons butter, melted
½ cup sugar
½ teaspoon vanilla extract
¼ cup evaporated milk
1 cup flaked coconut
1 cup chopped pecans

▸ Combine all ingredients in a bowl, stirring well.
▸ Spread Coconut Topping over cake.
▸ Broil 5 inches from heat 3 to 5 minutes or until coconut is browned. Watch closely because coconut will burn easily.
Yield: 12 to 16 servings

Italian Cream Cake

It's no surprise why this is everyone's favorite wedding cake.

Cake
½ cup butter or margarine
½ cup shortening
2 cups sugar
5 large eggs, separated
2 cups all-purpose flour
1 teaspoon baking soda
1 cup buttermilk
1 teaspoon vanilla extract
1⅓ cups flaked coconut
2 cups finely chopped pecans, divided

▸ Grease and flour 3 (9-inch) round cakepans.
▸ Beat butter and shortening at medium speed with an electric mixer 2 minutes or until creamy; gradually add sugar, beating 5 to 7 minutes. Add egg yolks, one at a time, beating just until yellow disappears after each addition.
▸ Combine flour and baking soda; add to butter mixture alternately with buttermilk, beginning and ending with flour mixture and beating at low speed just until blended after each addition. Stir in vanilla. Fold in coconut and 1 cup chopped nuts.
▸ Beat egg whites in a separate bowl at high speed until stiff peaks form. Fold into batter.
▸ Pour batter into prepared pans.
▸ Bake at 350° for 25 minutes or until a wooden pick inserted in center comes out clean. Remove from oven and let cool on wire racks 10 to 15 minutes.
▸ Remove cake layers from pans and let cool completely on wire racks.

Cream Cheese Frosting
1 (8-ounce) package cream cheese, softened
¼ cup butter or margarine, softened
1 (16-ounce) package powdered sugar
1 teaspoon vanilla extract

▸ Beat cream cheese and butter at medium speed with an electric mixer until creamy; add powdered sugar, beating well. Add vanilla and beat until smooth.
▸ Place one cake layer on a cake platter; spread with Cream Cheese Frosting. Top with second cake layer and spread with frosting. Top with third cake layer. Spread top and sides of cake with remaining frosting. Sprinkle top with remaining 1 cup chopped nuts.
Yield: 1 (3-layer) cake

Lemon Cake Squares

The combination of lemon and coconut is delicious.

1 (18.5-ounce) package lemon cake with pudding mix
½ cup butter, melted
½ cup chopped pecans
1 egg, lightly beaten
1 (3.5-ounce) can flaked coconut
3 eggs
1 (16-ounce) package powdered sugar
1 (8-ounce) package cream cheese, softened

▸ Coat a 13 x 9 x 2-inch pan with vegetable cooking spray.
▸ Combine first 4 ingredients in a bowl, mixing well. Press mixture into bottom of greased pan. Sprinkle coconut over top.
▸ Beat remaining 3 eggs, powdered sugar, and cream cheese at high speed with an electric mixer until creamy; pour over coconut.
▸ Bake at 325° for 45 minutes or until a wooden pick inserted in center comes out clean. Remove from oven and let cool completely on a wire rack.
▸ To serve, cut into squares.
Yield: 12 servings

Brickle Bar Cake

Truly, truly the most sinfully decadent way to eat a candy bar

1 (18.5-ounce) package Swiss chocolate or German chocolate cake mix
1 (14-ounce) can sweetened condensed milk
1 (12-ounce) jar caramel topping
1 (8-ounce) container frozen whipped topping, thawed
2 chocolate-covered butter brickle candy bars, crushed
  (we prefer Heath candy bars)

▸ Prepare cake mix according to package directions, baking in a greased 13 x 9 x 2-inch pan. Remove from oven and let cool on a wire rack 5 minutes.
▸ Punch holes all over cake using a large fork or a skewer. Pour sweetened condensed milk over top of cake. Pour caramel topping over cake. Let cake cool completely.
▸ Spread whipped topping over cake and sprinkle with crushed candy bars.
▸ Store cake in the refrigerator (best if made 1 or 2 days ahead).
Yield: 12 to 15 servings

Brown Sugar and Cream Dessert

Our guarantee-no leftovers!

1 cup firmly packed brown sugar
1 large egg, lightly beaten
1½ teaspoons vanilla extract
⅓ cup all-purpose flour
½ teaspoon baking soda
1 cup chopped pecans
1 pint whipping cream, whipped and divided

- Coat an 8-inch-square pan with vegetable cooking spray.
- To prepare cake, combine first 6 ingredients in a medium bowl, stirring well. Pour into greased pan.
- Bake at 325° for 25 minutes. Remove from oven and let cool 10 minutes on a wire rack. Remove from pan and cool completely.
- Crumble cake into a large bowl; fold in half of whipped cream. Spoon into an 8-inch square pan and chill thoroughly.
- To serve, cut cake and top each square with whipped cream.

Yield: 6 servings

Bishop Pound Cake

This pound cake has a rich lemon flavor.

1 cup butter, softened
½ cup shortening
3 cups sugar
5 large eggs
3 cups cake flour
½ teaspoon baking powder
1 cup milk
1 tablespoon lemon extract

- Grease and flour a 12-cup Bundt pan.
- Beat butter and shortening at medium speed with an electric mixer 2 minutes or until creamy; gradually add sugar, beating 5 to 7 minutes. Add eggs, one at a time, beating just until yellow disappears after each addition.
- Combine cake flour and baking powder; add to butter mixture alternately with milk, beginning and ending with flour mixture and beating at low speed just until blended after each addition. Stir in lemon extract.
- Pour batter into prepared pan.
- Bake at 350° for 50 to 60 minutes or until a wooden pick inserted in cake comes out clean. Remove from oven and let cool on a wire rack 15 minutes or until cake pulls away from sides of pan.
- Remove cake from pan and let cool completely on wire rack.

Yield: 1 (10-inch) cake

Buttermilk Pound Cake

Sifting the sugar creates a velvet-textured cake.

1 cup shortening
½ cup butter, softened
3 cups sugar
6 large eggs
3 cups cake flour
1 cup buttermilk
1 tablespoon vanilla extract

- Grease and flour a 10-inch Bundt or tube pan.
- Beat shortening and butter at medium speed with an electric mixer 2 minutes or until creamy.
- Sift sugar 3 times. Gradually add to shortening and beat at medium speed 10 minutes. Add eggs, one at a time, beating just until yellow disappears after each addition; beat 5 minutes.
- Sift cake flour 3 times; add flour to butter mixture alternately with buttermilk, beginning and ending with flour and beating at low speed just until blended after each addition. Stir in vanilla.
- Pour batter into prepared pan.
- Bake at 325° for 1 hour and 5 minutes or until a wooden pick inserted in cake comes out clean. Remove from oven and let cool in pan on a wire rack 15 minutes.
- Remove cake from pan and let cool completely on wire rack

Yield: 1 (10-inch) cake

NOTE: *A combination of 1 teaspoon vanilla extract, 1 teaspoon lemon extract, and 1 teaspoon almond extract may be substituted for 1 tablespoon vanilla extract, if desired.*

Elegant Chocolate Pound Cake

Sour cream and sweetened cocoa give this cake rich flavor.

1 cup butter or margarine, softened
2 ¼ cups sugar
1 ½ cups sweet ground chocolate and cocoa (we prefer Ghirardelli)
6 large eggs
2 ¼ cups plus 1 tablespoon all-purpose flour
¼ teaspoon baking soda
1 (8-ounce) container sour cream
2 teaspoons vanilla extract

- Grease and flour a 10-inch Bundt or tube pan.
- Beat butter at medium speed with an electric mixer 2 minutes or until creamy; gradually add sugar and chocolate and cocoa, beating 5 to 7 minutes. Add eggs, one at a time, beating just until yellow disappears after each addition.
- Combine flour and baking soda; add to butter mixture alternately with sour cream, beginning and ending with flour mixture and beating at low speed just until blended after each addition. Stir in vanilla.
- Pour batter into prepared pan.
- Bake at 325° for 1 hour and 20 minutes or until a wooden pick inserted in cake comes out clean. Remove from oven and let cool on a wire rack 10 to 15 minutes.
- Remove cake from pan and let cool completely on wire rack.

Yield: 1 (10-inch) cake

Brown Sugar Pound Cake

A no-fail crowd pleaser.

1½ cups butter or margarine, softened
1 (16-ounce) package light brown sugar
1 cup granulated sugar
5 large eggs
1 cup milk
1 teaspoon vanilla extract
3 cups all-purpose flour
1 teaspoon baking powder
½ teaspoon salt
1 cup chopped pecans (optional)

▸ Grease and flour a 10-inch Bundt or tube pan.
▸ Beat butter at medium speed with an electric mixer 2 minutes or until creamy; gradually add sugars, beating 5 to 7 minutes. Add eggs, one at a time, beating just until yellow disappears after each addition.
▸ Combine milk and vanilla in a small bowl.
▸ Combine flour, baking powder, and salt; add to butter mixture alternately with milk mixture, beginning and ending with flour mixture and beating at low speed just until blended after each addition. Fold in chopped nuts, if desired.
▸ Pour batter into prepared pan.
▸ Bake at 325° for 1 hour and 20 minutes or until a wooden pick inserted in cake comes out clean. Remove from oven and let cool on a wire rack 10 to 15 minutes.
▸ Remove cake from pan and let cool completely on wire rack.

Yield: 1 (10-inch) cake

Clarice's Rum Cake

One of our most requested recipes

Cake
1 cup chopped pecans
1 (18.5-ounce) package butter recipe yellow cake mix
(we prefer Duncan Hines)
1 (3¾-ounce) package vanilla instant pudding mix
½ cup rum
½ cup vegetable oil
½ cup water
4 large eggs

▸ Grease and flour a 10-inch Bundt or tube pan. Sprinkle nuts in bottom of pan.
▸ Combine cake mix and pudding mix in a large bowl; add rum, oil, ½ cup water, and eggs. Beat at medium speed with an electric mixer 2 minutes.
▸ Pour batter into prepared pan.
▸ Bake at 325° for 50 to 55 minutes or until a wooden pick inserted in cake comes out clean.
▸ Remove cake from oven and punch holes in the top with a large fork or a skewer. Pour hot rum glaze over cake. Let cake cool in the pan for 1 hour on a wire rack. Remove cake from pan and place on a serving plate.

Hot Rum Glaze
1 cup sugar
½ cup butter or margarine
¼ cup rum
¼ cup water

▸ Bring all ingredients to a boil in a medium saucepan; boil, stirring constantly, 3 to 4 minutes.
Yield: 16 servings

Apple Cake

Make this in the fall with the first apples of the season.

1¼ cups vegetable oil
2 cups sugar
3 large eggs
2 teaspoons vanilla extract
3 cups all-purpose flour
1 teaspoon baking soda
1 teaspoon salt
1 teaspoon ground cinnamon
3 large peeled apples, thinly sliced
1 cup chopped nuts

▸ Coat a 10-inch Bundt or tube pan with vegetable cooking spray.
▸ Beat oil and sugar at medium speed with an electric mixer until creamy; add eggs, one at a time, beating just until yellow disappears after each addition. Stir in vanilla.
▸ Sift together flour, soda, salt, and cinnamon; gradually add to creamed mixture, beating just until dry ingredients are moistened. Stir in apple slices and nuts.
▸ Pour batter into greased pan.
▸ Bake at 350° for 35 to 40 minutes or until a wooden pick inserted in cake comes out clean. Remove from oven and let cool on a wire rack 15 to 20 minutes. Remove cake from pan and let cool completely.
▸ Invert cake onto a serving plate.
Yield: 1 (10-inch) cake

Date-Wine Cake

Very good for gifts at Christmas, or anytime

Cake
2 cups boiling water
2 cups chopped dates
2 teaspoons baking soda
½ cup butter or margarine
2 cups sugar
2 large eggs
1 teaspoon vanilla extract
1 cup sweet sherry or sweet wine
3 cups all-purpose flour
1 tablespoon ground allspice
¼ teaspoon salt
2 cups chopped nuts
1 tablespoon all-purpose flour

▸ Grease 2 (9 x 5 x 3-inch) loaf pans or 1 (10-inch) tube pan.
▸ Pour 2 cups boiling water over dates in a bowl; stir well and let stand until cool. Stir in baking soda. Stir in vanilla and sherry.
▸ Beat butter and sugar at medium speed with an electric mixer 5 to 7 minutes or until creamy. Add eggs, one at a time, beating just until yellow disappears after each addition.
▸ Combine 3 cups flour, allspice, and salt. Add to creamed mixture alternately with date mixture, beginning and ending with flour mixture and beating at low speed just until blended after each addition.
▸ Combine nuts and 1 tablespoon flour, tossing to coat. Fold into batter.
▸ Spoon batter into greased pans.
▸ Bake at 350° for 1 hour or until a wooden pick inserted in center comes out clean. Remove from oven and let cool on a wire rack 10 to 15 minutes. remove cake from pan and cool completely.

Caramel Icing
½ cup butter
1 cup firmly packed dark brown sugar
1 cup granulated sugar
½ cup half-and-half

▸ Melt butter in a medium saucepan over medium heat; stir in sugars and half-and-half. Bring to a boil. Boil, stirring constantly, 2 minutes. Remove from heat and let cool.
▸ Beat icing at medium speed with an electric mixer until creamy.
▸ Spread icing on cake.
Yield: 2 loaves or 1 (10-inch) cake

Caramel Brownies

Using caramel ice-cream topping makes this recipe easier than unwrapping the caramel candies called for in the original recipe.

1 (18.5-ounce) package German chocolate cake mix
⅓ cup butter or margarine, softened
1 large egg
1 cup (6 ounces) semi-sweet chocolate morsels
½ cup chopped nuts, toasted
1 (12-ounce) jar hot caramel ice cream topping (not fat-free)
3 tablespoons all-purpose flour

▸ Grease a 13 x 9 x 2-inch pan.
▸ Beat first 3 ingredients at low speed with an electric mixer until crumbly. Set aside 1 cup mixture. Press remaining crumb mixture into greased pan.
▸ Bake at 350° for 8 to 10 minutes or until slightly puffy.
▸ Sprinkle chocolate morsels and nuts over baked crumb mixture.
▸ Combine caramel topping and flour, stirring well; pour over chocolate morsels and nuts. Sprinkle with reserved 1 cup crumb mixture.
▸ Bake at 350° for 15 to 20 minutes or until morsels are melted and caramel topping begins to bubble. Remove from oven and let cool on a wire rack.
▸ Cut into squares to serve.
Yield: 3 dozen

Chocolate Tea Bars

We often make these easy, delicious tea bars for League receptions.

2 large eggs
1 cup granulated sugar
2 tablespoons unsweetened cocoa
¼ cup butter, melted
½ cup all-purpose flour
1 teaspoon vanilla extract
Powdered sugar

▸ Grease and flour a 9-inch square pan.
▸ Beat eggs at medium speed with an electric mixer until light and fluffy; add granulated sugar and cocoa, beating well. Add butter, flour, and vanilla, beating until blended.
▸ Pour batter into prepared pan.
▸ Bake at 375° for 20 minutes or until a wooden pick inserted in center comes out clean. Remove from oven and let cool on a wire rack 10 minutes.
▸ Dust with powdered sugar.
▸ Cut into bars and serve.
Yield: 16 bars
NOTE: *When doubling ingredients, bake in 13 x 9 x 2-inch pan.*

Blonde Brownies

Moist and chewy with rich butterscotch flavor

6 tablespoons butter
I cup firmly packed dark brown sugar
2 large eggs
I teaspoon vanilla extract
⅔ cup all-purpose flour
I teaspoon baking powder
¼ teaspoon salt
½ cup chopped pecans

▸ Cook butter and brown sugar in a heavy saucepan over medium heat, stirring often, until sugar is melted and mixture is bubbly. Remove from heat and let cool slightly.
▸ Add eggs and vanilla to butter mixture, beating with a handheld mixer until blended.
▸ Combine flour, baking powder, and salt; add to butter mixture, beating just until thoroughly mixed. Stir in pecans.
▸ Spread batter in greased 8-inch square pan.
▸ Bake 30 minutes at 350° or until top is dry and a wooden pick inserted in center comes out almost clean. Remove from oven and let cool on a wire rack.
▸ Cut into 2-inch squares.
Yield: 16 brownies
VARIATION: For Coconut Butterscotch Brownies, add ½ cup shredded coconut to batter. Omit pecans, if desired.

Zesty Lemon-Nut Bars

The zest (or colored portion of the lemon rind) lends a rich flavor to the crust and the filling in these scrumptious lemon bars.

Bars
½ cup butter or margarine, softened
½ cup granulated sugar
Grated rind of 1 lemon, divided
1½ cups all-purpose flour, divided
1 cup firmly packed brown sugar
1 cup finely chopped walnuts or pecans
2 large eggs, lightly beaten
¼ teaspoon baking powder

▸ Beat butter, granulated sugar, and half of lemon rind at medium speed with an electric mixer until creamy; gradually stir in 1¼ cups flour to form a soft crumbly dough. Press dough evenly in the bottom of a 13 x 9 x 2-inch pan.
▸ Bake at 350° for 15 minutes.
▸ Combine remaining ¼ cup flour, remaining half of lemon rind, brown sugar, walnuts, eggs, and baking powder, stirring well. Spread over baked crust.
▸ Bake 20 minutes. Remove from oven and let cool on a wire rack.

Lemon Glaze
1 cup powdered sugar
1 tablespoon butter or margarine, softened
2 tablespoons fresh lemon juice

▸ Combine a small amount of powdered sugar and butter in a bowl, stirring to blend. Add lemon juice and remaining sugar, stirring until smooth.
▸ Thinly spread glaze over top while still hot.
▸ Cut into bars and serve.
Yield: 3 dozen

Jessica's Sweet Dreams

"My friends named these spicy, crisp chocolate chip cookies."

1 cup unsalted butter
½ cup firmly packed light brown sugar
1 large egg
1 teaspoon vanilla extract
2 cups all-purpose flour
1 teaspoon baking soda
½ teaspoon salt
1 teaspoon ground cinnamon
1 teaspoon ground ginger
1 cup pecans or walnuts, toasted and chopped
1 (12-ounce) package semi-sweet chocolate morsels
1½ cups powdered sugar

▸ Beat butter at medium speed with an electric mixer until creamy; add sugar, beating until well blended. Add egg and vanilla, beating until light and fluffy.
▸ Combine flour, baking soda, salt, cinnamon, and ginger; add to butter mixture, beating at low speed until well blended. Stir in nuts and chocolate morsels. Chill 1 to 2 hours or overnight.
▸ Shape dough into balls using a scant tablespoon of dough. Roll in powdered sugar and place on ungreased cookie sheets 1 inch apart.
▸ Bake at 350° for 12 to 15 minutes or until lightly browned. Remove from oven and let cool for 1 minute. Remove cookies from pans and let cool completely on wire racks.
Yield: about 7 dozen

Chocolate Clouds

You'll be in 7th heaven when you bite into the crackly outside and discover the moist, chewy inside.

3 ½ cups all-purpose flour
2 teaspoons baking powder
4 (1-ounce) unsweetened chocolate squares
1 cup butter or margarine
3 cups sugar
4 large eggs
1 teaspoon vanilla extract
1 teaspoon almond extract
2 cups assorted nuts (pecans, sliced almonds, and walnuts)
1 cup (6 ounces) semi-sweet chocolate morsels

- Whisk together flour and baking powder in a medium bowl. Set aside.
- Microwave chocolate and butter in a glass bowl at high 2 minutes. Remove from microwave and stir until blended.
- Combine chocolate mixture and sugar in a large bowl. Beat at medium speed with an electric mixer 1 minute or until blended; add eggs, one at a time, beating well after each addition. Add extracts, beating well.
- Add flour mixture to chocolate mixture, beating at low speed until blended. Stir in nuts and chocolate morsels. Cover and chill 1 hour.
- Shape dough into 1-inch balls and place 1 inch apart on ungreased cookie sheets.
- Bake at 350° for 12 minutes or until tops are cracked.
- Remove cookies from pans and let cool completely on wire racks.

Yield: 10 dozen

Molasses Cookies

These may be "old-fashioned" but they are still a hit.

¾ cup vegetable oil
1 cup sugar
1 large egg, lightly beaten
¼ cup molasses
2 cups all-purpose flour
¼ teaspoon salt
2 teaspoons baking soda
2 teaspoons ground cinnamon
2 teaspoons ground cloves
2 teaspoons ground ginger
Granulated sugar

▸ Beat oil and 1 cup sugar at medium speed with an electric mixer until creamy; add egg and molasses, beating well.
▸ Sift together flour, salt, baking soda, cinnamon, cloves, and ginger; add to creamed mixture, beating at low speed until well blended.
▸ Divide dough in half; wrap each portion in plastic wrap and chill 6 to 8 hours or overnight.
▸ Working with 1 portion at a time, shape dough into balls using 1 tablespoon of dough. Roll in sugar and place on ungreased cookie sheets 2 inches apart.
▸ Bake at 375° for 10 to 12 minutes or until crisp and lightly browned. Remove from oven and let cool on wire racks.
Yield: 4 dozen

Angel Crisp Tea Cakes

"Out of this world"

½ cup shortening
½ cup butter or margarine
1 cup granulated sugar
1 cup powdered sugar
1 large egg, lightly beaten
1 teaspoon vanilla extract
4 cups all-purpose flour
1 teaspoon baking soda
1 teaspoon salt
1 teaspoon cream of tartar
Granulated sugar

▸ Beat first 4 ingredients at medium speed with an electric mixer until creamy; add egg and vanilla, beating well.
▸ Sift together flour, baking soda, salt, and cream of tartar; gradually add to butter mixture, beating at low speed until well blended (dough will be soft). Chill 10 to 15 minutes.
▸ Roll dough into balls using 1 teaspoon of dough. Place on buttered cookie sheets. Dip a fork in water and press dough to flatten. Sprinkle tops of dough with granulated sugar.
▸ Bake at 350° for 12 minutes or until light golden. Remove from pan and cool completely on wire rack.
Yield: 4 dozen

Iced Butter Cookies

Children's little thumbs are perfect for helping with these pretty tea party cakes.

Cookies
1 cup butter or margarine, softened
½ cup sifted powdered sugar
2 cups all-purpose flour
1 tablespoon vanilla extract
1 cup finely chopped pecans (optional)

▸ Beat butter at medium speed with an electric mixer until creamy; gradually add powdered sugar, beating well. Add flour, beating well. Stir in vanilla and, if desired, pecans.
▸ Shape dough into 1-inch balls and place about 2 inches apart on ungreased cookie sheets. Press thumb in center of each cookie to make an indentation.
▸ Bake at 350° for 15 to 17 minutes or until light golden (do not brown). Remove from oven and let cool on wire racks.
▸ Fill cookie indentations with Praline Filling or Rainbow Icing.
Yield: about 3 dozen

Praline Filling
½ cup butter or margarine
1 cup firmly packed brown sugar
Dash of salt
½ cup evaporated milk
2 cups sifted powdered sugar
½ teaspoon vanilla extract

▸ Melt butter in a medium saucepan over medium heat; add brown sugar and salt and bring to a boil. Boil, stirring constantly, 2 minutes. Remove from heat.
▸ Stir evaporated milk into butter mixture and bring to a boil. Boil 2 minutes or until a candy thermometer registers 232° (thread stage). Remove from heat and let cool to lukewarm.
▸ Add powdered sugar and vanilla to mixture, beating with a wooden spoon until smooth.
Yield: about 1½ cups
OR

Rainbow Icing
½ (16-ounce) package powdered sugar
1 teaspoon vanilla extract
Desired color liquid food coloring
1 tablespoon water

▸ Stir together all ingredients in a bowl, adding water to desired spreading consistency.

Index

Cultural Arts League
Center for Cultural Arts
P.O. Box 1507
Gadsden, AL 35902

Please send _____ copy(ies)   @ $18.95 each _____

    Shipping and handling   @ $ 4.00 each _____

Alabama residents add 8% sales tax   @ $ 1.52 each _____

Name _____

Address _____

City _____ State _____ Zip _____

Make checks payable to Cultural Arts League

- -

Cultural Arts League
Center for Cultural Arts
P.O. Box 1507
Gadsden, AL 35902

Please send _____ copy(ies)   @ $18.95 each _____

    Shipping and handling   @ $ 4.00 each _____

Alabama residents add 8% sales tax   @ $ 1.52 each _____

Name _____

Address _____

City _____ State _____ Zip _____

Make checks payable to Cultural Arts League

- -

Cultural Arts League
Center for Cultural Arts
P.O. Box 1507
Gadsden, AL 35902

Please send _____ copy(ies)   @ $18.95 each _____

    Shipping and handling   @ $ 4.00 each _____

Alabama residents add 8% sales tax   @ $ 1.52 each _____

Name _____

Address _____

City _____ State _____ Zip _____

Make checks payable to Cultural Arts League